TWENTIETH CENTURY
INTERPRETATIONS

MAYNARD MACK, *Series Editor*
Yale University

NOW AVAILABLE
Collections of Critical Essays
ON

ADVENTURES OF HUCKLEBERRY FINN

ALL FOR LOVE

THE FROGS

THE GREAT GATSBY

HENRY V

THE ICEMAN COMETH

SAMSON AGONISTES

THE SOUND AND THE FURY

TWELFTH NIGHT

WALDEN

TWENTIETH CENTURY INTERPRETATIONS
OF

HAMLET

TWENTIETH CENTURY INTERPRETATIONS
OF
HAMLET

A Collection of Critical Essays

Edited by

DAVID BEVINGTON

Prentice-Hall, Inc. A SPECTRUM BOOK *Englewood Cliffs, N. J.*

To Helen

Current printing (last number):
10   9   8   7   6   5   4   3

Contents

Introduction

by David Bevington

It is appropriate that for modern critics *Hamlet* should be Shake-speare's greatest dramatic enigma, for misunderstanding is the un-avoidable condition of Hamlet's quest for certainties. Not only is he baffled by riddling visions and by commands seemingly incapable of fulfillment, but he is the victim of misinterpretation by those around him. Well may the dying Hamlet urge his friend Horatio to "report me and my cause aright To the unsatisfied," for no one save Horatio has caught more than a glimpse of Hamlet's true situation. We as omniscient audience, hearing the inner thoughts of Claudius as well as of Hamlet and learning of Polonius' or Laertes' secret plot-tings with the king, should remember that we know vastly more than the play's characters, and that this discrepancy between our view-point and theirs is one of Shakespeare's richest sources of dramatic irony.

The basis of misunderstanding, and hence of Hamlet's estrange-ment, is the secret murder. Claudius, before the opening of the play, has slain his brother by such cunning means that no mortal suspects him—not even at first the sorrowing Hamlet, until the ghost's horrid news awakens the unstated imaginings of Hamlet's "prophetic soul." Ever the masterly politician, Claudius has engineered his own suc-cession to the throne in place of his nephew Hamlet not by usurpa-tion, but by full consent of the Danish court. Claudius is to out-ward appearances an apt choice. Polonius and other reputedly sage counselors welcome the rule of one so fit for soothing public utterance and for pragmatic foreign diplomacy. Claudius, to his credit, disarms the threat of invasion by young Fortinbras of Norway that hangs so ominously over the beginning of the play. The king's instructions to the ambassadors, Voltemand and Cornelius, are seasoned by years of hard political calculation. His marriage with the dead king's widow, even if technically incestuous, gives an aura of continuity to the new reign. It is without conscious irony that Rosencrantz and Guildenstern, appointed guardians of the unpredictable Hamlet, echo great Elizabethan commonplaces in their defense of legitimate monarchical authority. The life of their king is threatened, and they

1

know that majesty "Dies not alone, but like a gulf doth draw What's near it with it." Ophelia, ignorant of the murder, cannot fathom the sudden and vindictive hostility of one who had professed love to her "In honorable fashion." Passively becoming part of a scheme designed, as far as she can tell, to help Hamlet recover his wits, Ophelia instead loses her own. Her brother Laertes' rashness is similarly made plausible, even if it cannot be condoned, by his total unawareness of Hamlet's reasons for opposing the king and Polonius. Only in the final scene does Laertes perceive too late that he is caught like "a woodcock to mine own springe," and is "justly killed with mine own treachery."

Hamlet by contrast is from the first a stranger in the court of Denmark, despite his position as son of the dead king and as "most immediate to our throne" after Claudius. An outsider, he returns from years of advanced study at Wittenberg to a society he considers too worldly and corrupted. It is "as a stranger" that he shares with Horatio a secret knowledge of there being "more things in heaven and earth" than are dreamt of in mere philosophy. He upbraids the Danish for their heavy drinking, a custom better broken than observed. Well before he learns of the murder, he spurns the hypocrisy of meats baked for a funeral coldly furnishing forth the wedding festivities of his uncle-father and aunt-mother. He knows not "seems." Hamlet's innate antipathy to false appearances, exacerbated by his mother's overhasty wedding, helps explain both his suspicion of others' motives and their bafflement at his seeming caprice. Claudius is sincere in his attempts to make a reconciliation with a young prince who is cherished by his mother and beloved by the common people. Gertrude can only suppose that her son is offended by her infidelity to the memory of her dead husband—for she like the others apparently knows nothing of the actual murder—and so she fondly hopes that Hamlet will marry Ophelia and settle down into tranquil domesticity. Polonius, whose routine it is to make intelligence reports on potential troublemakers, finds an easy clue to Hamlet's "madness" in Ophelia's rejection of him. Rosencrantz and Guildenstern are equally convinced that Hamlet's malady is political—his lack of "advancement" to the throne.

These answers formulated by the Danish court to explain Hamlet's mystery are not unusually obtuse. They are the guesswork of shrewd observers who merely lack knowledge of Hamlet's awful truth. The answers are in fact all valid in their limited ways. Gertrude may well fear that Hamlet's distemper needs no other explanation than "His father's death and our o'erhasty marriage." Hamlet becomes a mirror reflecting the conscience of each observer, and the guilty marriage is what Gertrude sees in herself. "You go not till I set you up a glass," he exhorts his mother, "Where you may see the inmost part of you." Claudius, having reason to surmise more than most, has most to fear. Polonius creates a fantasy of love based on his own stratagems in matchmaking, but his fiction only exaggerates Hamlet's real obsession with feminine frailty. When Rosencrantz and Guildenstern speak of ambition, they are talking mostly about themselves; yet Hamlet does belatedly admit, at least to Horatio, that Claudius has "Popped in between th' election and my hopes." All these explorations of motive have meaning to us who know the prime cause.

What Hamlet objects to is the oversimplification and the prying that destroys the integrity of his whole and complex being. "If circumstances lead me, I will find Where truth is hid, though it were hid indeed Within the center," opines Polonius, irritating us as well as Hamlet with his officious claims to omniscience. Similarly, Hamlet is incensed at Rosencrantz and Guildenstern for supposing they can sound his inner nature more easily than one might play a recorder. "You would play upon me, you would seem to know my stops, you would pluck out the heart of my mystery," he accuses them, adding with a pun, "though you can fret me, you cannot play upon me." Hamlet here expresses one of the most profound bases of our identification with his loneliness. Every human being is unique and believes that others can never fully understand or appreciate him. And every human being experiences some perverse delight in this proof of the world's callousness.

If, in his turn, Hamlet also indulges in amateur motive-hunting and so alienates those who would seek an accommodation with him, he merely typifies in dramatically heightened form a human tendency to prefer estrangement. His is, after all, an extraordinary situation. It is plausible that a young man so suddenly deprived of his father and confronted with evidence of his mother's fleshly weakness should generalize upon the depravity of the human condition, even in himself. Moreover Hamlet is intellectually inclined to searching out hidden meanings in events. The cold watch on the tower at midnight, the appearance of the ghost, and the cruel contrast between the ugly truth here revealed and the empty glitter of the court, impel him to the conclusion that "All is not well." Humanity itself, so potentially noble in reason and godlike in its infinite faculties, dissolves in his imaginative vision into a quintessence of dust. The goodly frame of nature becomes a "foul and pestilent congregation of vapors." Man's very being, infected by some "vicious mole [blemish] of nature" inherited involuntarily at birth, overthrows "the pales and forts of reason" and thereby corrupts the whole. Men are prisoners of their appetites, helpless to achieve the goodness so mockingly revealed by their philosophic quest for the ideal.

Overwhelmed by this negation, Hamlet can only suspect others of inconstancy. He need not overhear Polonius' scheme of using Ophelia to bait a trap, for Hamlet is predisposed to expect collusion. He has tested womankind by the behavior of his mother and knows them all to be false. "Frailty, thy name is woman," he concludes in his first soliloquy. If Hamlet senses something amiss in Ophelia's suddenly returning his love letters to him, he only guesses intuitively what in fact Polonius has said to his daughter. She must learn to play a wary game to treat Hamlet's advances as "springes to catch woodcocks," and to regard his holy vows as devices to undo her virginity. Princes are expected to claim their rights as libertines, in Polonius' complacent vision of the universal lewdness in human nature. However cruel in its treatment of Ophelia, Hamlet's response is in kind. He becomes afflicted by the ruthless mores prevailing in Denmark, because he has a distasteful business to accomplish. Only too late can he publicly acknowledge that he loved the fair Ophelia, stressing the tragedy of misunderstanding that has obliged him to destroy what he most cherished. Similarly he acknowledges too late his real respect for Laertes and his regret at their fatal enmity. These two men might in better times have loved one another. A chief source of the melancholic mood in *Hamlet* derives from this sense of lost opportunity.

Hamlet does grow harsh and cynical like his opponents. Yet he never ceases to tax himself as severely as he does the others. He is indeed much like them. Polonius, his seeming opposite in so many ways, is, like Hamlet, an inveterate punster. To whom else but Polonius should Hamlet direct the taunt of "Words, words, words"? The aged counselor recalls that in his youth he "suffered much extremity for love, very near this," and he has been an actor at the university. Polonius too has advice for the players: "Seneca cannot be too heavy, nor Plautus too light." When Hamlet jibes at "so capital a calf" enacting Julius Caesar, killed in the Capitol, he reinforces the parallel to his own playacting and anticipates the slaying of Polonius behind the arras. If Hamlet is a mirror to the others, the reflection works both ways.

Perhaps the central reflection of this sort is between Hamlet and Claudius. Not only has Claudius taken Hamlet's mother and his crown, but Claudius is a prisoner of circumstance, burdened with a guilty responsibility, unable to rid himself of his enemy by forthright action. Hamlet is a constant danger to the king, and yet no plausible grounds can at first be discovered for proceeding against Hamlet. Only after the "mousetrap" play do both of them know that action is imperative; and yet both of them find their subsequent moves thwarted by unforeseen circumstances and deceptive appearances. Claudius is the only character other than Hamlet whom we overhear in soliloquy, and we learn on this occasion that Claudius too cannot resolve seemingly impossible alternatives. How is he to retain the queen, whom he has won by sinful lust, and at the same time free his tortured soul of guilt? It is ironically appropriate that Claudius' prayer should offer Hamlet his sole opportunity for successful revenge, an opportunity lost because Claudius gives the semblance of being in a state of contrition. Ultimately Hamlet and Claudius slay one another in a finale that neither could have anticipated.

Sharing the weaknesses of those he reviles, Hamlet turns his most unsparing criticisms upon himself. The appalling contrast between his uncle and father reminds him of the contrast between himself and Hercules—although when the fit of action is upon him he is as hardy as "The Nemean lion's nerve." "We are arrant knaves all," he warns Ophelia, "believe none of us." Although more honest than most, Hamlet accounts himself unworthy to have been born: "I am very proud, revengeful, ambitious, with more offenses at my beck than I have thoughts to put them in, imagination to give them shape, or time to act them in." His self-remonstrances repeatedly sound the note of generalization. He is like other men in being "a breeder of sinners," and he includes all mankind in his dilemma of action: "conscience doth make cowards of us all." Paradoxically, although he characterizes himself as a vengeful man too full of sinful deeds, he reproaches himself most often for his failure to take arms against his sea of troubles. "O, what a rogue and peasant slave am I!" The son of a dear father murdered, he can only unpack his heart with words. Is this the result, he ponders, of "Bestial oblivion, or some craven scruple Of thinking too precisely on th' event"? Is he allowing himself to be paralyzed into inaction by his introspection, obscuring "the native hue of resolution" with "the pale cast of thought"? If Hamlet asks this question and has no clear answer, we need not be surprised that it has tantalized modern criticism.

Several limits can be placed upon the search for an explanation of Hamlet's apparent hesitation to avenge. He is not ineffectual under ordinary circumstances. Elizabethan theories of melancholy did not suppose the sufferer to be made necessarily inactive. Hamlet has a deserved reputation in Denmark for manliness and princely demeanor. He keeps up his fencing practice and will "win at the odds" against Laertes. He threatens with death those who would restrain him from speaking with the ghost—even his friend Horatio—and stabs the concealed Polonius unflinchingly. On the sea voyage to England he boards a pirate ship singlehanded in the grapple, after having arranged without remorse for the deaths of Rosencrantz and Guildenstern. In light of these deeds, Hamlet's self-accusations are signs of burning impatience in one who would surely act if he could. His contemplations of suicide follow similarly upon his frustrated perceptions of an impasse; suicide is a logical alternative when action appears meaningless, even if suicide must be rejected on grounds of Christian faith.

Such considerations turn our attention from Hamlet's supposed "fault" or "tragic flaw" to the context of his world and its philosophical absurdities. Wherein can he find trust and certitude? "Say, why is this?" he begs his father's ghost. "Wherefore? what should we do?" According to popular Elizabethan belief, both Catholic and Protestant, spirits from the dead could indeed "assume a pleasing shape," in order to abuse a person in Hamlet's vulnerable frame of mind and so lead him to damnation. If Hamlet's plan to test the ghost's message by the "mousetrap" play causes him to wonder about his own cowardice and inconstancy, the accusations are directed against the impotent and self-contradictory nature of his situation.

Even after the clear revelation of Claudius' guilt at Hamlet's play, the exact plan of action remains anything but clear. Hamlet must face the ghost once again to explain why he "lets go by Th' important acting of your dread command"; yet his purpose in confronting Gertrude with her weakness is the laudable one of returning her to at least an outward custom of virtue. Having earlier been uncertain of appearances in the apparition of his father, Hamlet now is deceived and hence delayed in his resolve by the semblance of Claudius' praying. Hamlet has always believed that heavenly justice will prevail among men: "Foul deeds will rise, Though all the earth o'erwhelm them, to men's eyes." Murder, though it have no tongue, "will speak With most miraculous organ." Nevertheless, man's perception of that divine revelation, and his role in aiding the course of justice, are obscured by man's own corruption and blindness. Whenever Hamlet moves violently, he moves in error. Horatio, in summing up the play, speaks tellingly of "accidental judgments, casual slaughters," and of "purposes mistook Fall'n on th' inventors' heads." The judgment applies to Hamlet as to Laertes and Claudius. Hamlet has already realized that he must pay the price of heaven's displeasure for killing Polonius, just as Polonius himself has paid the price for his own meddling. "Heaven hath pleased it so, To punish me with this, and this with me." Such fitting reciprocity can be brought about only by the far-reaching arm of providence. The engineer must be "Hoist with his own petar."

Hamlet quests for clear action, but it mockingly eludes him. He yearns to be like Fortinbras, proceeding resolutely in a military action against Poland, but perceives at the same time that Fortinbras, in his absurd campaign for a patch of barren ground, for "this straw," for "an eggshell," must risk two thousand souls and a kingly fortune. The tomb in which these vast numbers will be laid to rest for no purpose anticipates the graveyard of Yorick and Ophelia, reaching back in its universal history to King Alexander and to Adam, the first gravemaker. The magnificent Alexander and imperious Caesar, renowned for exploits greater than those of Fortinbras, are now turned to clay and can serve only to stop a bunghole. This generalized vision of earthly vanity is no mere excuse for Hamlet's irresolution, for it shows the benign intention of providence in achieving a coherence beyond the grasp of human comprehension. Fortinbras of course succeeds politically where Hamlet must fail, and is chosen by Hamlet to restore Denmark to political health; but to acknowledge this discrepancy is merely to confirm the distance between order on earth and the higher perfection which Hamlet conceives.

It is only when Hamlet has come to terms with the absurdity of human action, and has resigned himself to the will of heaven, that a way is opened for him at last. Fittingly, he achieves this detachment in the company of Horatio. However much Horatio's philosophic skepticism may limit his own ability to perceive those "things in heaven and earth" that Hamlet would have him observe, Horatio remains the companion from whom Hamlet has most to learn. Hamlet can trust his friend not to angle for advancement, or to reveal the terrible secret of royal murder. Best of all, Horatio is "As one in suff'ring all that suffers nothing, A man that Fortune's buffets and rewards Hast ta'en with equal thanks." The true stoic, choosing to "suffer The slings and arrows of outrageous fortune" rather than futilely oppose them, is proof against the insidious temptation of worldly success as well as against disappointment. While other courtiers gravitate to Claudius with his seemingly magical formula for prospering, and so lose themselves in worldliness, Horatio sides with one who is sacrificed and so receives his commission as guardian of the truth.

Like Hamlet, Horatio believes that death is a felicity, and even tries to take his own life. Yet he accepts his duty "in this harsh world" to draw his breath in pain to tell Hamlet's story. He acquiesces in Hamlet's conclusion that "Our indiscretion sometime serves us well When our deep plots do pall." Horatio may beg his friend to postpone the fencing match if his mind misgives, because Horatio, unlike Hamlet, never achieves the full sense of exultation in anticipating unknown events; yet Horatio knows finally that Hamlet was right. "Praised be rashness!" says Hamlet. The train of events, leading by subterranean complexities from Hamlet's apparently un-

wise slaying of Polonius, ends in all that was "Devoutly to be wished"
—not least in Hamlet's own surcease from pain and incertitude, by
means of a soldier's death rather than a suicide's. "If it be not now,
yet it will come. The readiness is all." Hamlet is indeed the recipient
of a "special providence," and becomes for us the type of hero whose
death is needed to confirm not only the tragic dignity of man's
struggle against misfortune, but also the wisdom of the gods in or-
daining such a pattern.

Structurally, the play of *Hamlet* is dominated by the pairing of
various characters to reveal one as the "foil" of another. "I'll be
your foil, Laertes," says Hamlet, punning on the resemblance that
elsewhere he seriously acknowledges: "by the image of my cause I
see The portraiture of his." Laertes has returned from abroad to
help celebrate the royal wedding; he loses a father by violent means
and seeks vengeance. The common people, usually loyal to young
Hamlet, are roused to a new hero-worship upon the occasion of
Laertes' second return to Denmark. "Choose we! Laertes shall be
king!" Ophelia too has been deprived of a father; so has Fortinbras.
Hamlet stands at the center of these comparisons, the proper focus
of the play. He is the composite man, graced as Ophelia observes
with "The courtier's, soldier's, scholar's, eye, tongue, sword." From
each comparison we see another facet of his complex being, and
another danger from extremes which he must learn to avoid.

We have already seen the similarities of Claudius and Polonius
to Hamlet. Laertes, burdened with a responsibility like Hamlet's,
moves to expedient action without scruple. He turns at first on
Claudius, who is technically innocent of Polonius' death. The popular
insurrection will simultaneously feed Laertes' revenge and his ambition. Presented with untested and partial evidence concerning
Hamlet's part in Polonius' murder, Laertes would "cut his throat
i' th' church." He does in fact grapple with Hamlet in the graveyard,
striking the first blow and prompting Hamlet to assure his rival
that he is not "splenitive and rash." More than that, Laertes con-
nives with the king in underhanded murder; it is Laertes who thinks
of poisoning the sword's point with an unction already bought of
a mountebank. This poison recalls the murder of King Hamlet and
the murder of Gonzago. Purposes of this sort can only return to
plague the inventor.

Ophelia's response to her father's death is quite opposite to her
brother's, but no less a reflection on Hamlet's dilemma. Her mind
is not equal to the buffets of fortune, and she will not draw her
breath in pain. She wanders from her mad sexual fantasies to muddy
death. If the gravediggers and the priest are to be believed, her
dreams, once she has "shuffled off this mortal coil," must give us

pause. Fortinbras is a more positive figure, since he withholds his
hand against the Danes in vengeance of his father, choosing to in-
herit the Danish throne by diplomatic patience and canny timing
rather than by battle; but at best his counsel is "greatly to find quarrel
in a straw When honor's at the stake." Horatio's philosophy of
stoical indifference to fortune offers the greatest consolation to
Hamlet, and yet it cannot predict the important outcome by which
divinity will reveal itself in the fall of a sparrow.

Characters also serve as foils to one another as well as to Hamlet.
Gertrude wishfully sees in Ophelia the blushing bride of Hamlet,
innocently free from the compromises and surrenders which Gertrude
has never mastered the strength to escape. Yet to Hamlet, Ophelia
is no better than another Gertrude: both are tender of heart but
submissive to the will of importunate men, and so are forced into
uncharacteristic vices. Both would be other than what they are, and
both receive Hamlet's exhortations to begin repentance by abstaining
from pleasure. "Get thee to a nunnery"; "Assume a virtue if you have
it not."

Hamlet's language puts much stress on the pun and other forms
of wordplay. This habit of speech, so often a lapse in taste, is here
appropriate to the portrayal of a keen mind tortured by alternatives.
In his first appearance, Hamlet offers a double meaning in each of
his answers to the king and queen. Because he is now both Claudius'
cousin and son, Hamlet is "A little more than kin, and less than
kind"—too incestuously close, and yet neither kindly disposed nor
bound by the legitimate ties of nature ("kind") as is a son to his
true father. Denying that the clouds of sorrow still hang on him,
Hamlet protests he is "too much in the sun"—basking more than
he wishes in the king's unctuous favor, and so, more a "son" than
he thinks right. To his mother, who must cling to her worldly belief that the death of husbands and fathers is "common" or commonplace and hence to be taken in one's stride, Hamlet wryly counters:
"Ay, madam, it is common." It is low, coarse, revolting.

In each double meaning Hamlet pierces to the heart of seeming.
Mere forms, moods, or shapes of grief cannot denote him truly; he
must discover the "absolute" in meaning and so quibbles with words
and their deceptive masks. When his friend Horatio says to Hamlet
"There's no offense," meaning conventionally that Horatio is not
affronted by Hamlet's wild and whirling words on the battlements,
Hamlet is quick to remember the larger issue of morality in Denmark:
"Yes, by Saint Patrick, but there is, Horatio, And much offense too."
When Polonius, merely to encourage small talk, asks Hamlet "What
is the matter" that he reads, Hamlet will have no chitchat. What is
the matter "Between who?" Small wonder that Hamlet exults in

the gravedigger's playing upon the idiotic and profound question of the ownership of a grave: this one belongs to one that is not a woman, but who *was* a woman. "How absolute the knave is!" This digger is the same natural philosopher who has explicated the three branches of acting—"to act, to do, and to perform."

In patterns of images, *Hamlet* employs metaphors of clothes, of acting, and of disease. Again, like the wordplay, these images aim at the discrepancy between a handsome exterior and corrupted inner being. Hamlet decries inky cloaks, "windy suspiration of forced breath," and other appurtenances of mourning, even though he himself is still dressed in black and so is visibly separated from the wedding party at court. Polonius reveals his trust in the game of preserving appearances by his worldly advice to his son: "the apparel oft proclaims the man." This maxim loses its irony when quoted out of context. Osric's sterile infatuation with clothes and mannerisms serves as one last reminder of the world's hypocrisy that Hamlet can now regard with almost comic detachment. Hamlet as actor is a master of many styles, frighting Ophelia in his fouled stockings, ungartered "As if he had been loosèd out of hell," or composing jingling love doggerel to be read solemnly in open court, or declaiming in an outmoded and stilted tragical rhetoric on the massacre of Troy. He is critical of the professional players' fondness for exaggerated gestures, interpolated bawdry, and overblown rhetoric, because they must aid him in a subtle resemblance of truth designed to lay bare a human conscience. They must hold "the mirror up to nature, to show virtue her own feature, scorn her own image, and the very age and body of the time his form and pressure." Acting becomes a process of reality in uncovering the veneer of court life.

At the center of this revelation is the figure of the dead King Hamlet, whose magnificent person has been "barked about Most lazar-like with vile and loathsome crust." Denmark, and the world itself, is "an unweeded garden That grows to seed. Things rank and gross in nature Possess it merely." Hamlet's role is that of a physician who must lance the ulcerous sore or corruption, by putting Claudius "to his purgation" or speaking "daggers" to his mother in order to cure her soul. He must reveal Claudius to Gertrude for what her husband truly is, "a mildewed ear Blasting his wholesome brother." Without such exposure, Gertrude's complacency "will but skin and film the ulcerous place Whiles rank corruption, mining all within, Infects unseen." The poison that precipitates the action of the play, both a metaphor of disease and an actual evil, must be transformed into a providential weapon ending the lives of Claudius, Gertrude, and Laertes, as well as Hamlet.

Shakespeare wrote *Hamlet* in 1600 or 1601, when he was thirty-six years old. It was his first major tragedy, although *Julius Caesar* may have been slightly earlier, and it ushered in the decade of the great tragedies: *Othello, Macbeth, King Lear, Antony and Cleopatra,* and *Coriolanus.* During the 1590's Shakespeare had excelled as a writer of English history plays and romantic comedies. Before he turned to *Hamlet,* he had offered virtually his final statement in historical form with *Henry V,* summarizing his examination of kingship begun in the *Henry VI* plays and *Richard III* and pursued in *Richard II* and *Henry IV.* Similarly in comedy, the years around 1595 to 1599 had seen the culmination of his "festive" comic vein with *The Merchant of Venice, Much Ado About Nothing, As You Like It,* and *Twelfth Night.*

Shakespeare was, in 1600, an accomplished and eminently practical man of the stage, already recognized by contemporaries as England's chief playwright. Coming from an artisan background like so many of his fellow-writers—Jonson, Spenser, Marlowe—this young man had eventually joined the Lord Chamberlain's men and had helped them to achieve an unquestioned primacy in London's financially successful theater. His considerable earnings, invested chiefly in Stratford property, enabled him to retire comfortably in 1611 and rejoin his family in their permanent home. He began his career as an actor. Only in his later years was he able to give up acting in order to devote primary attention to writing. Shakespeare was an actor-sharer of the company, dividing profits of the gate and assisting in the productions. He knew the actors as friends and wrote for their talents, although he and they rose above the limitations that such a closed arrangement might suggest. Richard Burbage played Hamlet, and he doubtlessly graced the role with a masculine and lofty forcefulness that had become a byword for him among London viewers. The company's theater, the Globe, resembled an earlier theater built by Burbage's father to serve as England's first permanent public stage. The Globe featured a large rectangular platform projected into the center of an innyard-like arena so that spectators could witness the action from most sides. A curtained area in the rear and an upper balcony were used sparingly; most action took place on stage, without scenery and in full daylight (even for the appearance of ghosts).

As a working member of a commercial enterprise, Shakespeare did not hesitate to use in his plays whatever source material lay at hand: Italianate novellas, chronicle histories of England by Grafton, Hall, and Holinshed, and older plays. A *Hamlet* seems to have existed prior to Shakespeare's own. It was a revenge play, perhaps the work of Thomas Kyd, and employed the familiar contrivances of this popular Senecan tradition: ghosts seeking revenge, "mousetrap" plays, the antic disposition of the avenger, and a bloody finale. Kyd's own *Spanish Tragedy,* in the late 1580's, set a standard for the genre, and Shakespeare had made a clumsy attempt at revenge tragedy in *Titus Andronicus* (ca. 1593). Also at hand were the nondramatic legends of Hamlet, especially the twelfth century *Historia Danica* of Saxo Grammaticus, and a free redaction of the legend by Belleforest in 1576.

Whatever his sources—and they all strike us as comparatively savage and immature—Shakespeare achieved a transformation in *Hamlet* that was exquisitely attuned to the sophisticated questionings of his own era. *Hamlet* stands at the dividing point between two great periods of Shakespeare's creativity, one chiefly optimistic and one overwhelmingly tragic. Although we must guard against easy biographical and historical answers to this change in emphasis, it remains true that the 1590's saw a great outpouring of English patriotic fervor in drama, whereas the 1600's turned away from history plays almost entirely. The public companies flourished in the 1590's; thereafter theatrical tastes shifted increasingly to the private stage of the boy actors. Shakespeare comments indirectly in *Hamlet* on the rivalry between the public and private theaters, observing with dismay that the boys "cry out on the top of question" and have obliged the public actors to travel more in the provinces. Shakespeare's company, renamed the King's Men after 1603, was obliged to seek an accommodation with the private theaters. After King James's accession to the throne and his uncompromising stance toward Puritanism, the great London theatrical public began to fall away and was displaced by a smaller, richer, and more courtly clientele. Literary satire grew fashionable. John Donne's metaphysical poetry, begun in the late 1590's, caught the mood of doubt. Perhaps it is this timely urging in *Hamlet* that has recommended it especially to modern audiences similarly bemused by the absurdity of human action. The play's hero stands between a Christian, medieval world of faith, and one of skeptical uncertainty. His universal dilemma becomes our own.

PART ONE

Interpretations

Shakespeare's Tragic Period—*Hamlet*

by *A. C. Bradley*

Let us first ask ourselves what we can gather from the play, immediately or by inference, concerning Hamlet as he was just before his father's death. And I begin by observing that the text does not bear out the idea that he was one-sidedly reflective and indisposed to action. Nobody who knew him seems to have noticed this weakness. Nobody regards him as a mere scholar who has "never formed a resolution or executed a deed." In a court which certainly would not much admire such a person he is the observed of all observers. Though he has been disappointed of the throne everyone shows him respect; and he is the favorite of the people, who are not given to worship philosophers. Fortinbras, a sufficiently practical man, considered that he was likely, had he been put on, to have proved most royally. He has Hamlet borne by four captains "like a soldier" to his grave; and Ophelia says that Hamlet *was* a soldier. If he was fond of acting, an aesthetic pursuit, he was equally fond of fencing, an athletic one: he practised it assiduously even in his worst days. [1] So far as we can conjecture from what we see of him in those bad days, he must normally have been charmingly frank, courteous and kindly to everyone, of whatever rank, whom he liked or respected, but by no means timid or deferential to others; indeed, one would gather that he was rather the reverse, and also that he was apt to be decided and even imperious if thwarted or interfered with. He must always have been fearless,—in the play he appears insensible to fear of any ordinary kind. And, finally, he must have been quick and impetuous in action; for it is downright impossible that the man we see rushing after the Ghost, killing Polonius, dealing with the King's commission on the ship, boarding the pirate, leaping into

"*Shakespeare's Tragic Period*—Hamlet" by *A. C. Bradley. From* Shakespearean Tragedy *(London: Macmillan & Co., Ltd., 1903), pp. 108-120. Reprinted by permission of St. Martin's Press, Inc. This selection is section 3 of Lecture 3.*

[1] He says so to Horatio, whom he has no motive for deceiving (v. ii. 218). His contrary statement (II. ii. 308) is made to Rosencrantz and Guildenstern.

the grave, executing his final vengeance, could *ever* have been shrinking or slow in an emergency. Imagine Coleridge doing any of these things!

If we consider all this, how can we accept the notion that Hamlet's was a weak and one-sided character? "Oh, but he spent ten or twelve years at a University!" Well, even if he did, it is possible to do that without becoming the victim of excessive thought. But the statement that he did rests upon a most insecure foundation.

Where then are we to look for the seeds of danger?

1. Trying to reconstruct from the Hamlet of the play, one would not judge that his temperament was melancholy in the present sense of the word; there seems nothing to show that; but one would judge that by temperament he was inclined to nervous instability, to rapid and perhaps extreme changes of feeling and mood, and that he was disposed to be, for the time, absorbed in the feeling or mood that possessed him, whether it were joyous or depressed. This temperament the Elizabethans would have called melancholic; and Hamlet seems to be an example of it, as Lear is of a temperament mixedly choleric and sanguine. And the doctrine of temperaments was so familiar in Shakespeare's time—as Burton, and earlier prose-writers, and many of the dramatists show—that Shakespeare may quite well have given this temperament to Hamlet consciously and deliberately. Of melancholy in its developed form, a habit, not a mere temperament, he often speaks. He more than once laughs at the passing and half-fictitious melancholy of youth and love; in Don John in *Much Ado* he had sketched the sour and surly melancholy of discontent; in Jaques a whimsical self-pleasing melancholy; in Antonio in the *Merchant of Venice* a quiet but deep melancholy, for which neither the victim nor his friends can assign any cause. [2] He gives to Hamlet a temperament which would not develop into melancholy unless under some exceptional strain, but which still involved a danger. In the play we see the danger realized, and find a melancholy quite unlike any that Shakespeare had as yet depicted, because the temperament of Hamlet is quite different.

2. Next, we cannot be mistaken in attributing to the Hamlet of earlier days an exquisite sensibility, to which we may give the name "moral," if that word is taken in the wide meaning it ought to bear. This, though it suffers cruelly in later days, as we saw in criticizing the sentimental view of Hamlet, never deserts him; it makes all his

---

[2] The critics have labored to find a cause, but it seems to me Shakespeare simply meant to portray a pathological condition; and a very touching picture he draws. Antonio's sadness, which he describes in the opening lines of the play, would never drive him to suicide, but it makes him indifferent to the issue of the trial, as all his speeches in the trial-scene show.

cynicism, grossness and hardness appear to us morbidities, and has an inexpressibly attractive and pathetic effect. He had the soul of the youthful poet as Shelley and Tennyson have described it, an unbounded delight and faith in everything good and beautiful. We know this from himself. The world for him was *wie am ersten Tag*— "this goodly frame the earth, this most excellent canopy the air, this brave o'erhanging firmament, this majestical roof fretted with golden fire." And not nature only: "What a piece of work is a man! how noble in reason! how infinite in faculty! in form and moving how express and admirable! in action how like an angel! in apprehension how like a god!" This is no commonplace to Hamlet; it is the language of a heart thrilled with wonder and swelling into ecstasy.

Doubtless it was with the same eager enthusiasm he turned to those around him. Where else in Shakespeare is there anything like Hamlet's adoration of his father? The words melt into music whenever he speaks of him. And, if there are no signs of any such feeling towards his mother, though many signs of love, it is characteristic that he evidently never entertained a suspicion of anything unworthy in her,—characteristic, and significant of his tendency to see only what is good unless he is forced to see the reverse. For we find this tendency elsewhere, and find it going so far that we must call it a disposition to idealize, to see something better than what is there, or at least to ignore deficiencies. He says to Laertes, "I loved you ever," and he describes Laertes as a "very noble youth," which he was far from being. In his first greeting of Rosencrantz and Guildenstern, where his old self revives, we trace the same affectionateness and readiness to take men at their best. His love for Ophelia, too, which seems strange to some, is surely the most natural thing in the world. He saw her innocence, simplicity and sweetness, and it was like him to ask no more; and it is noticeable that Horatio, though entirely worthy of his friendship, is, like Ophelia, intellectually not remarkable. To the very end, however clouded, this generous disposition, this "free and open nature," this unsuspiciousness survive. They cost him his life; for the King knew them, and was sure that he was too "generous and free from all contriving" to "peruse the foils." To the very end, his soul, however sick and tortured it may be, answers instantaneously when good and evil are presented to it, loving the one and hating the other. He is called a sceptic who has no firm belief in anything, but he is never sceptical about *them*.

And the negative side of his idealism, the aversion to evil, is perhaps even more developed in the later Hamlet than in the character I am trying to reconstruct. It is intensely characteristic. Nothing, I believe, is to be found elsewhere in Shakespeare (unless in the rage of the disillusioned idealist Timon) of quite the same kind as Hamlet's disgust at his uncle's drunkenness, his loathing of his mother's sensuality, his astonishment and horror at her shallowness, his contempt for everything pretentious or false, his indifference to everything merely external. This last characteristic appears in his choice of the friend of his heart, and in a certain impatience of distinctions of rank or wealth. When Horatio calls his father "a goodly king," he answers, surely with an emphasis on "man,"

> He was a man, take him for all in all,
> I shall not look upon his like again.

He will not listen to talk of Horatio being his "servant." When the others speak of their "duty" to him, he answers, "Your love, as mine to you." He speaks to the actor precisely as he does to an honest courtier. He is not in the least a revolutionary, but still, in effect, a king and a beggar are all one to him. He cares for nothing but human worth, and his pitilessness towards Polonius and Osric and his "school-fellows" is not wholly due to morbidity, but belongs in part to his original character.

Now, in Hamlet's moral sensibility there undoubtedly lay a danger. Any great shock that life might inflict on it would be felt with extreme intensity. Such a shock might even produce tragic results. And, in fact, *Hamlet* deserves the title "tragedy of moral idealism" quite as much as the title "tragedy of reflection."

3. With this temperament and this sensibility we find, lastly, in the Hamlet of earlier days, as of later, intellectual genius. It is chiefly this that makes him so different from all those about him, good and bad alike, and hardly less different from most of Shakespeare's other heroes. And this, though on the whole the most important trait in his nature, is also so obvious and so famous that I need not dwell on it at length. But against one prevalent misconception I must say a word of warning. Hamlet's intellectual power is not a specific gift, like a genius for music or mathematics or philosophy. It shows itself, fitfully, in the affairs of life as unusual quickness of perception, great agility in shifting the mental attitude, a striking rapidity and fertility in resource; so that, when his natural belief in others does not make him unwary, Hamlet easily sees through them and masters them, and no one can be much less like the typical helpless dreamer. It shows itself in conversation chiefly in the form of wit or humor; and, alike in conversation and in soliloquy, it shows itself in the form of imagination quite as much as in that of thought in the stricter sense. Further, where it takes the latter shape, as it very often does, it is not philosophic in the technical meaning of

the word. There is really nothing in the play to show that Hamlet ever was "a student of philosophies," unless it be the famous lines which, comically enough, exhibit this supposed victim of philosophy as its critic:

> There are more things in heaven and earth, Horatio,
> Than are dreamt of in your philosophy.[3]

His philosophy, if the word is to be used, was, like Shakespeare's own, the immediate product of the wondering and meditating mind; and such thoughts as that celebrated one, "There is nothing either good or bad but thinking makes it so," surely needed no special training to produce them. Or does Portia's remark, "Nothing is good without respect," *i.e.*, out of relation, prove that she had studied metaphysics?

Still Hamlet had speculative genius without being a philosopher, just as he had imaginative genius without being a poet. Doubtless in happier days he was a close and constant observer of men and manners, noting his results in those tables which he afterwards snatched from his breast to make in wild irony his last note of all, that one may smile and smile and be a villain. Again and again we remark that passion for generalization which so occupied him, for instance, in reflections suggested by the King's drunkenness that he quite forgot what it was he was waiting to meet upon the battlements. Doubtless, too, he was always considering things, as Horatio thought, too curiously. There was a necessity in his soul driving him to penetrate below the surface and to question what others took for granted. That fixed habitual look which the world wears for most men did not exist for him. He was for ever unmaking his world and rebuilding it in thought, dissolving what to others were solid facts, and discovering what to others were old truths. There were no old truths for Hamlet. It is for Horatio a thing of course that there's a divinity that shapes our ends, but for Hamlet it is a discovery hardly won. And throughout this kingdom of the mind, where he felt that man, who in action is only like an angel, is in apprehension like a god, he moved (we must imagine) more than content, so that even in his dark days he declares he could be bounded in a nutshell and yet count himself a king of infinite space, were it not that he had bad dreams.

If now we ask whether any special danger lurked *here*, how shall we answer? We must answer, it seems to me, "Some danger, no doubt, but, granted the ordinary chances of life, not much." For, in the first

[3] Of course "your" does not mean Horatio's philosophy in particular. "Your" is used as the Gravedigger uses it when he says that "your water is a sore decayer of your . . . dead body."

place, that idea which so many critics quietly take for granted—the idea that the gift and the habit of meditative and speculative thought tend to produce irresolution in the affairs of life—would be found by no means easy to verify. Can you verify it, for example, in the lives of the philosophers, or again in the lives of men whom you have personally known to be addicted to such speculation? I cannot. Of course, individual peculiarities being set apart, absorption in *any* intellectual interest, together with withdrawal from affairs, may make a man slow and unskilful in affairs; and doubtless, individual peculiarities being again set apart, a mere student is likely to be more at a loss in a sudden and great practical emergency than a soldier or a lawyer. But in all this there is no difference between a physicist, a historian, and a philosopher; and again, slowness, want of skill, and even helplessness are something totally different from the peculiar kind of irresolution that Hamlet shows. The notion that speculative thinking specially tends to produce *this* is really a mere illusion.

In the second place, even if this notion were true, it has appeared that Hamlet did *not* live the life of a mere student, much less of a mere dreamer, and that his nature was by no means simply or even one-sidedly intellectual, but quite healthily active. Hence, granted the ordinary chances of life, there would seem to be no great danger in his intellectual tendency and his habit of speculation; and I would go further and say that there was nothing in them, taken alone, to unfit him even for the quite extraordinary call that was made upon him. In fact, if the message of the Ghost had come to him within a week of his father's death, I see no reason to doubt that he would have acted on it as decisively as Othello himself, though probably after a longer and more anxious deliberation. And therefore the Schlegel-Coleridge view (apart from its descriptive value) seems to me fatally untrue, for it implies that Hamlet's procrastination was the normal response of an overspeculative nature confronted with a difficult practical problem.

On the other hand, under conditions of a peculiar kind, Hamlet's reflectiveness certainly might prove dangerous to him, and his genius might even (to exaggerate a little) become his doom. Suppose that violent shock to his moral being of which I spoke; and suppose that under this shock, any possible action being denied to him, he began to sink into melancholy; then, no doubt, his imaginative and generalizing habit of mind might extend the effects of this shock through his whole being and mental world. And if, the state of melancholy being thus deepened and fixed, a sudden demand for difficult and decisive action in a matter connected with the melancholy arose, this state might well have for one of its symptoms an endless and futile mental dissection of the required deed. And, finally, the futility of this process, and the shame of his delay, would further weaken him and enslave him to his melancholy still more. Thus the speculative habit would be *one* indirect cause of the morbid state which hindered action; and it would also reappear in a degenerate form as one of the *symptoms* of this morbid state.

Now this is what actually happens in the play. Turn to the first words Hamlet utters when he is alone; turn, that is to say, to the place where the author is likely to indicate his meaning most plainly. What do you hear?

> O, that this too too solid flesh would melt,
> Thaw and resolve itself into a dew!
> Or that the Everlasting had not fix'd
> His canon 'gainst self-slaughter! O God! God!
> How weary, stale, flat and unprofitable,
> Seem to me all the uses of this world!
> Fie on't! ah fie! 'tis an unweeded garden,
> That grows to seed; things rank and gross in nature
> Possess it merely.

Here are a sickness of life, and even a longing for death, so intense that nothing stands between Hamlet and suicide except religious awe. And what has caused them? The rest of the soliloquy so thrusts the answer upon us that it might seem impossible to miss it. It was not his father's death; that doubtless brought deep grief, but mere grief for some one loved and lost does not make a noble spirit loathe the world as a place full only of things rank and gross. It was not the vague suspicion that we know Hamlet felt. Still less was it the loss of the crown: for though the subserviency of the electors might well disgust him, there is not a reference to the subject in the soliloquy, nor any sign elsewhere that it greatly occupied his mind. It was the moral shock of the sudden ghastly disclosure of his mother's true nature, falling on him when his heart was aching with love, and his body doubtless was weakened by sorrow. And it is essential, however disagreeable, to realize the nature of this shock. It matters little here whether Hamlet's age was twenty or thirty: in either case his mother was a matron of mature years. All his life he had believed in her, we may be sure, as such a son would. He had seen her not merely devoted to his father, but hanging on him like a newly wedded bride, hanging on him

> As if increase of appetite had grown
> By what it fed on.

He had seen her following his body "like Niobe, all tears." And
then within a month—"O God! a beast would have mourned longer"
—she married again, and married Hamlet's uncle, a man utterly con-
temptible and loathsome in his eyes; married him in what to
Hamlet was incestuous wedlock; [4] married him not for any reason
of state, nor even out of old family affection, but in such a way that
her son was forced to see in her action not only an astounding
shallowness of feeling but an eruption of coarse sensuality, "rank
and gross," [5] speeding posthaste to its horrible delight. Is it possible
to conceive an experience more desolating to a man such as we have
seen Hamlet to be; and is its result anything but perfectly natural?
It brings bewildered horror, then loathing, then despair of human
nature. His whole mind is poisoned. He can never see Ophelia in
the same light again: she is a woman, and his mother is a woman:
if she mentions the word "brief" to him, the answer drops from his
lips like venom, "as woman's love." The last words of the soliloquy,
which is *wholly* concerned with this subject, are,

> But break, my heart, for I must hold my tongue!

He can do nothing. He must lock in his heart, not any suspicion of
his uncle that moves obscurely there, but that horror and loathing;
and if his heart ever found relief, it was when those feelings, mingled
with the love that never died out in him, poured themselves forth
in a flood as he stood in his mother's chamber beside his father's
marriage bed.[6]

If we still wonder, and ask why the effect of this shock should be
so tremendous, let us observe that *now* the conditions have arisen
under which Hamlet's highest endowments, his moral sensibility
and his genius, become his enemies. A nature morally blunter would

4 This aspect of the matter leaves *us* comparatively unaffected, but Shakespeare
evidently means it to be of importance. The Ghost speaks of it twice, and Hamlet
thrice (once in his last furious words to the King). If, as we must suppose, the marriage was universally admitted to be incestuous, the corrupt acquiescence of the
court and the electors to the crown would naturally have a strong effect on Hamlet's
mind.

5 It is most significant that the metaphor of this soliloquy reappears in Hamlet's
adjuration to his mother (III. iv. 150):

> Repent what's past; avoid what is to come;
> And do not spread the compost on the weeds
> To make them ranker.

6 If the reader will now look at the only speech of Hamlet's that precedes the
soliloquy, and is more than one line in length—the speech beginning "Seems,
madam! nay, it *is*"—he will understand what, surely, when first we come to it,
sounds very strange and almost boastful. It is not, in effect, about Hamlet himself at
all; it is about his mother (I do not mean that it is intentionally and consciously so;
and still less that she understood it so).

have felt even so dreadful a revelation less keenly. A slower and more limited and positive mind might not have extended so widely through its world the disgust and disbelief that have entered it. But Hamlet has the imagination which, for evil as well as good, feels and sees all things in one. Thought is the element of his life, and his thought is infected. He cannot prevent himself from probing and lacerating the wound in his soul. One idea, full of peril, holds him fast, and he cries out in agony at it, but is impotent to free himself ("Must I remember?" "Let me not think on't"). And when, with the fading of his passion, the vividness of this idea abates, it does so only to leave behind a boundless weariness and a sick longing for death.

And this is the time which his fate chooses. In this hour of uttermost weakness, this sinking of his whole being towards annihilation, there comes on him, bursting the bounds of the natural world with a shock of astonishment and terror, the revelation of his mother's adultery and his father's murder, and, with this, the demand on him, in the name of everything dearest and most sacred, to arise and act. And for a moment, though his brain reels and totters, his soul leaps up in passion to answer this demand. But it comes too late. It does but strike home the last rivet in the melancholy which holds him bound.

> The time is out of joint! O cursed spite
> That ever I was born to set it right,—

so he mutters within an hour of the moment when he vowed to give his life to the duty of revenge; and the rest of the story exhibits his vain efforts to fulfil this duty, his unconscious self-excuses and unavailing self-reproaches, and the tragic results of his delay.

Hamlet and His Problems

by T. S. Eliot

Few critics have ever admitted that *Hamlet* the play is the primary problem, and Hamlet the character only secondary. And Hamlet the character has had an especial temptation for that most dangerous type of critic: the critic with a mind which is naturally of the creative order, but which through some weakness in creative power exercises itself in criticism instead. These minds often find in Hamlet a vicarious existence for their own artistic realization. Such a mind had Goethe, who made of Hamlet a Werther; and such had Coleridge, who made of Hamlet a Coleridge; and probably neither of these men in writing about Hamlet remembered that his first business was to study a work of art. The kind of criticism that Goethe and Coleridge produced, in writing of Hamlet, is the most misleading kind possible. For they both possessed unquestionable critical insight, and both make their critical aberrations the more plausible by the substitution —of their own Hamlet for Shakespeare's—which their creative gift effects. We should be thankful that Walter Pater did not fix his attention on this play.

Two writers of our time, Mr. J. M. Robertson and Professor Stoll of the University of Minnesota, have issued small books which can be praised for moving in the other direction. Mr. Stoll performs a service in recalling to our attention the labors of the critics of the seventeenth and eighteenth centuries,[1] observing that

> they knew less about psychology than more recent Hamlet critics, but they were nearer in spirit to Shakespeare's art; and as they insisted on the importance of the effect of the whole rather than on the importance

[1] I have never, by the way, seen a cogent refutation of Thomas Rymer's objections to *Othello*.

of the leading character, they were nearer, in their old-fashioned way, to the secret of dramatic art in general.

Qua work of art, the work of art cannot be interpreted; there is nothing to interpret; we can only criticize it according to standards, in comparison to other works of art; and for "interpretation" the chief task is the presentation of relevant historical facts which the reader is not assumed to know. Mr. Robertson points out, very pertinently, how critics have failed in their "interpretation" of *Hamlet* by ignoring what ought to be very obvous: that *Hamlet* is a stratification, that it represents the efforts of a series of men, each making what he could out of the work of his predecessors. The *Hamlet* of Shakespeare will appear to us very differently if, instead of treating the whole action of the play as due to Shakespeare's design, we perceive his *Hamlet* to be superposed upon much cruder material which persists even in the final form.

We know that there was an older play by Thomas Kyd, that extraordinary dramatic (if not poetic) genius who was in all probability the author of two plays so dissimilar as the *Spanish Tragedy* and *Arden of Feversham;* and what this play was like we can guess from three clues: from the *Spanish Tragedy* itself, from the tale of Belleforest upon which Kyd's *Hamlet* must have been based, and from a version acted in Germany in Shakespeare's lifetime which bears strong evidence of having been adapted from the earlier, not from the later, play. From these three sources it is clear that in the earlier play the motive was a revenge motive simply; that the action or delay is caused, as in the *Spanish Tragedy*, solely by the difficulty of assassinating a monarch surrounded by guards; and that the "madness" of Hamlet was feigned in order to escape suspicion, and successfully. In the final play of Shakespeare, on the other hand, there is a motive which is more important than that of revenge, and which explicitly "blunts" the latter; the delay in revenge is unexplained on grounds of necessity or expediency; and the effect of the "madness" is not to lull but to arouse the king's suspicion. The alteration is not complete enough, however, to be convincing. Furthermore, there are verbal parallels so close to the *Spanish Tragedy* as to leave no doubt that in places Shakespeare was merely *revising* the text of Kyd. And finally there are unexplained scenes—the Polonius-Laertes and the Polonius-Reynaldo scenes—for which there is little excuse; these scenes are not in the verse style of Kyd, and not beyond doubt in the style of Shakespeare. These Mr. Robertson believes to be scenes in the original play of Kyd reworked by a third hand, perhaps Chapman, before Shakespeare touched the play. And he concludes, with very strong show of reason, that the original play of Kyd was, like certain other revenge plays, in two parts of five acts each. The upshot of Mr. Robertson's examination is, we believe, irrefragable: that Shakespeare's *Hamlet,* so far as it is Shakespeare's, is a play dealing with the effect of a mother's guilt upon her son, and that Shakespeare was unable to impose this motive successfully upon the "intractable" material of the old play.

Of the intractability there can be no doubt. So far from being Shakespeare's masterpiece, the play is most certainly an artistic failure. In several ways the play is puzzling, and disquieting as is none of the others. Of all the plays it is the longest and is possibly the one on which Shakespeare spent most pains; and yet he has left in it superfluous and inconsistent scenes which even hasty revision should have noticed. The versification is variable. Lines like

> Look, the morn, in russet mantle clad,
> Walks o'er the dew of yon high eastern hill,

are of the Shakespeare of *Romeo and Juliet.* The lines in Act V. Sc. ii,

> Sir, in my heart there was a kind of fighting
> That would not let me sleep . . .
> Up from my cabin,
> My sea-gown scarf'd about me, in the dark
> Grop'd I to find out them: had my desire;
> Finger'd their packet;

are of his quite mature. Both workmanship and thought are in an unstable position. We are surely justified in attributing the play, with that other profoundly interesting play of "intractable" material and astonishing versification, *Measure for Measure,* to a period of crisis, after which follow the tragic successes which culminate in *Coriolanus.* *Coriolanus* may be not as "interesting" as *Hamlet,* but it is, with *Antony and Cleopatra,* Shakespeare's most assured artistic success. And probably more people have thought *Hamlet* a work of art because they found it interesting, than have found it interesting because it is a work of art. It is the "Mona Lisa" of literature.

The grounds of *Hamlet's* failure are not immediately obvious. Mr. Robertson is undoubtedly correct in concluding that the essential emotion of the play is the feeling of a son towards a guilty mother:

> [Hamlet's] tone is that of one who has suffered tortures on the score of his mother's degradation. . . . The guilt of a mother is an almost intolerable motive for drama, but it had to be maintained and emphasized to supply a psychological solution, or rather a hint of one.

This, however, is by no means the whole story. It is not merely the "guilt of a mother" that cannot be handled as Shakespeare handled the suspicion of Othello, the infatuation of Antony, or the pride of Coriolanus. The subject might conceivably have expanded into a tragedy like these, intelligible, self-complete, in the sunlight. *Hamlet,* like the sonnets, is full of some stuff that the writer could not drag to light, contemplate, or manipulate into art. And when we search for this feeling, we find it, as in the sonnets, very difficult to localize. You cannot point to it in the speeches; indeed, if you examine the two famous soliloquies you see the versification of Shakespeare, but a content which might be claimed by another, perhaps by the author of the *Revenge of Bussy d'Ambois,* Act V. Sc. i. We find Shakespeare's Hamlet not in the action, not in any quotations that we might select, so much as in an unmistakable tone which is unmistakably not in the earlier play.

The only way of expressing emotion in the form of art is by finding an "objective correlative"; in other words, a set of objects, a situation, a chain of events which shall be the formula of that *particular* emotion; such that when the external facts, which must terminate in sensory experience, are given, the emotion is immediately evoked. If you examine any of Shakespeare's more successful tragedies, you will find this exact equivalence; you will find that the state of mind of Lady Macbeth walking in her sleep has been communicated to you by a skilful accumulation of imagined sensory impressions; the words of Macbeth on hearing of his wife's death strike us as if, given the sequence of events, these words were automatically released by the last event in the series. The artistic "inevitability" lies in this complete adequacy of the external to the emotion; and this is precisely what is deficient in *Hamlet.* Hamlet (the man) is dominated by an emotion which is inexpressible, because it is in *excess* of the facts as they appear. And the supposed identity of Hamlet with his author is genuine to this point: that Hamlet's bafflement at the absence of objective equivalent to his feelings is a prolongation of the bafflement of his creator in the face of his artistic problem. Hamlet is up against the difficulty that his disgust is occasioned by his mother, but that his mother is not an adequate equivalent for it; his disgust envelops and exceeds her. It is thus a feeling which he cannot understand; he cannot objectify it, and it therefore remains to poison life and obstruct action. None of the possible actions can satisfy it; and nothing that Shakespeare can do with the plot can express Hamlet for him. And it must be noticed that the very nature of the *données* of the problem precludes objective equivalence. To have heightened the criminality of Gertrude would have been to provide the formula for a totally different emotion in Hamlet; it is just *because* her character is so negative and insignificant that she arouses in Hamlet the feeling which she is incapable of representing.

The "madness" of Hamlet lay to Shakespeare's hand; in the earlier play a simple ruse, and to the end, we may presume, understood as a ruse by the audience. For Shakespeare it is less than madness and more than feigned. The levity of Hamlet, his repetition of phrase, his puns, are not part of a deliberate plan of dissimulation, but a form of emotional relief. In the character Hamlet it is the buffoonery of an emotion which can find no outlet in action; in the dramatist it is the buffoonery of an emotion which he cannot express in art. The intense feeling, ecstatic or terrible, without an object or exceeding its object, is something which every person of sensibility has known; it is doubtless a subject of study for pathologists. It often occurs in adolescence: the ordinary person puts these feelings to sleep, or trims down his feelings to fit the business world; the artist keeps them alive by his ability to intensify the world to his emotions. The Hamlet of Laforgue is an adolescent; the Hamlet of Shakespeare is not, he has not that explanation and excuse. We must simply admit that here Shakespeare tackled a problem which proved too much for him. Why he attempted it at all is an insoluble puzzle; under compulsion of what experience he attempted to express the inexpressibly horrible, we cannot ever know. We need a great many facts in his biography; and we should like to know whether, and when, and after or at the same time as what personal experience, he read Montaigne, II. xii, *Apologie de Raimond Sebond*. We should have, finally, to know something which is by hypothesis unknowable, for we assume it to be an experience which, in the manner indicated, exceeded the facts. We should have to understand things which Shakespeare did not understand himself.

Place-Structure and Time-Structure

by Harley Granville-Barker

There is both a place-structure and a time-structure in *Hamlet*. The place-structure depends upon no exact localization of scenes. The time-structure answers to no scheme of act division. But each has its dramatic import.

The action of *Hamlet* is concentrated at Elsinore; and this though there is much external interest, and the story abounds in journeys. As a rule in such a case, unless they are mere messengers, we travel with the travellers. But we do not see Laertes in Paris, nor, more surprisingly, Hamlet among the pirates; and the Norwegian affair is dealt with by hearsay till the play is two-thirds over. This is not done to economize time, or to leave space for more capital events. Scenes in Norway or Paris or aboard ship need be no longer than the talk of them, and Hamlet's discovery of the King's plot against him is a capital event. Shakespeare is deliberately concentrating his action at Elsinore. When he does at last introduce Fortinbras he stretches probability to bring him and his army seemingly to its very suburbs; and, sooner than that Hamlet should carry the action abroad with him, Horatio is left behind there to keep him in our minds. On the other hand he still, by allusion, makes the most of this movement abroad which he does not represent; he even adds to our sense of it by such seemingly superfluous touches as tell us that Horatio has journeyed from Wittenberg, that Rosencrantz and Guildenstern have been "sent for"—and even the Players are travelling.

The double dramatic purpose is plain. Here is a tragedy of inaction; the center of it is Hamlet, who is physically inactive too, has "foregone all custom of exercises," will not "walk out of the air," but only, book in hand, for "four hours together, here in the lobby." The concentration at Elsinore of all that happens enhances the impression of this inactivity, which is enhanced again by the sense also given us of

"Place-Structure and Time-Structure" by Harley Granville-Barker. From Prefaces to Shakespeare: Hamlet *(Princeton: Princeton University Press, Illus. edn., 1965), pp. 38-46. Copyright 1946 by Princeton University Press; illus. edn. copyright © 1963 by the Trustees of the Author; notes to the illustrations copyright © 1963 by M. St. Clare Byrne. Reprinted by permission of the Princeton University Press and B. T. Batsford, Ltd., London. Footnotes are omitted.*

the constant coming and going around Hamlet of the busier world without. The place itself, moreover, thus acquires a personality, and even develops a sort of sinister power; so that when at last Hamlet does depart from it (his duty still unfulfilled) and we are left with the conscience-sick Gertrude and the guilty King, the mad Ophelia, a Laertes set on his own revenge, among a

> people muddied
> Thick and unwholesome in their thoughts and whispers . . .

we almost seem to feel it, and the unpurged sin of it, summoning him back to his duty and his doom. Shakespeare has, in fact, here adopted something very like unity of place; upon no principle, but to gain a specific dramatic end.

He turns time to dramatic use also, ignores or remarks its passing, and uses clock or calendar or falsifies or neglects them just as it suits him.

The play opens upon the stroke of midnight, an ominous and "dramatic" hour. The first scene is measured out to dawn and gains importance by that. In the second Hamlet's "not two months dead" and "within a month . . ." give past events convincing definition, and his "to-night . . . to-night . . . upon the platform twixt eleven and twelve" a specific imminence to what is to come. The second scene upon the platform is also definitely measured out from midnight to near dawn. This framing of the exordium to the tragedy within a precise two nights and a day gives a convincing life-likeness to the action, and sets its pulse beating rhythmically and arrestingly.

But now the conduct of the action changes, and with this the treatment of time. Hamlet's resolution—we shall soon gather—has paled, his purpose has slackened. He passes hour upon hour pacing the lobbies, reading or lost in thought, oblivious apparently to time's passing, lapsed—he himself supplies the phrase later—"lapsed in time." So Shakespeare also for a while tacitly ignores the calendar. When Polonius despatches Reynaldo we are not told whether Laertes has already reached Paris. Presumably he has, but the point is left vague. The Ambassadors return from their mission to Norway. They must, one would suppose, have been absent for some weeks; but again, we are not told. Why not insist at once that Hamlet has let a solid two months pass and made no move, instead of letting us learn it quite incidentally later? There is more than one reason for not doing so. If the fact is explicitly stated that two months separate this scene from the last, that breaks our sense of a continuity in the action; a thing not to be done if it can be avoided, for this sense of continuity helps to sustain illusion, and so to hold us attentive. An alternative would be to insert a scene or more dealing with occurrences during these two months, and thus bridge the gap in time. But a surplusage of incidental matter is also and always to be avoided. Polonius' talk to Reynaldo, Shakespeare feels, is relaxation and distraction enough; for with that scene only half-way through he returns to his main theme.

He could, however, circumvent such difficulties if he would. His capital reason for ignoring time hereabouts is that Hamlet is ignoring it, and he wants to attune the whole action—and us—to Hamlet's mood. He takes advantage of this passivity; we learn to know our man, as it were, at leisure. Facet after facet of him is turned to us. Polonius and Rosencrantz and Guildenstern are mirrors surrounding and reflecting him. His silence as he sits listening to the players—and we, as we listen, watch him—admits us to closer touch with him. And when, lest the tension of the action slacken too much in this atmosphere of timelessness, the clock must be restarted, a simple, incidental, phrase or two is made to serve.

It is not until later that Shakespeare, by a cunning little stroke, puts himself right—so to speak—with the past. *The Murder of Gonzago* is about to begin when Hamlet says to Ophelia:

> Look you, how cheerfully my mother looks, and my father died within 's two hours.

—to be answered

> Nay, 'tis twice two months, my lord.

There is the calendar re-established; unostentatiously, and therefore with no forfeiting of illusion. Yet at that moment we are expectantly attentive, so every word will tell. And it is a stroke of character too. For here is Hamlet, himself so lately roused from his obliviousness, gibing at his mother for hers.

But the use of time for current effect has begun again, and very appropriately, with Hamlet's fresh impulse to action, and his decision, reached while he listens abstractedly to the Player's speech, to test the King's guilt:

> we'll hear a play to-morrow. Dost thou hear me, old friend; can you play the Murder of Gonzago? . . . we'll ha't to-morrow night.

We do not yet know what is in his mind. But from this moment the pressure and pace of the play's action are to increase; and the brisk "to-morrow" and "to-morrow night" help give the initial impulse. The increase is progressive. In the next scene the play is no longer to be "to-morrow" but "to-night." The King, a little later, adds to the pressure. When he has overheard Hamlet with Ophelia:

> I have in quick determination
> Thus set it down; he shall with speed to England. . . .

And this—still progressively—becomes, after the play-scene and the killing of Polonius:

> The sun no sooner shall the mountains touch
> But we will ship him hence. . . .

After the spell of timelessness, then, we have an exciting stretch of the action carried through in a demonstrated day and a night. But the time-measure is not in itself the important thing. It is only used to validate the dramatic speed, even as was timelessness to help slow the action down.

After this comes more ignoring of the calendar, though the dramatic purpose in doing so is somewhat different. The scene which follows Hamlet's departure opens with the news of Ophelia's madness. We are not told how much time has elapsed. For the moment the incidental signs are against any pronounced gap. Polonius has already been buried, but "in hugger-mugger"; and Ophelia, whom we last saw smiling and suffering under Hamlet's torture, might well have lost her wits at the very news that her father had been killed, and that the man she loved had killed him. But suddenly Laertes appears in full-blown rebellion. With this it is clear why the calendar has been ignored. Shakespeare has had to face the same sort of difficulty as before. Let him admit a definite gap in time, realistically required for the return of Laertes and the raising of the rebellion, and he must either break the seeming continuity of the action, or build a bridge of superfluous matter and slacken a tension already sufficiently slackened by the passing of the Fortinbras army and Hamlet's "How all occasions . . ." soliloquy. So he takes a similar way out, ignoring incongruities, merely putting in the King's mouth the passing excuse that Laertes

> is *in secret* come from France . . .
> And wants not buzzers to infect his ear
> With pestilent speeches of his father's death . . .

—an excuse which would hardly bear consideration if we were allowed to consider it; but it is at this very instant that the tumult begins. And once again the technical maneuvering is turned to dramatic account. The surprise of Laertes' appearance, the very inadequacy and confusion of its explanation, and his prompt success, are in pertinent contrast to Hamlet's elaborate preparations—and his failure.

Only with news of Hamlet do we revert to the calendar, and then with good reason. By setting a certain time for his return, the tension of the action is automatically increased. First, in the letter to Horatio, the past is built up:

> Ere we were *two days* old at sea, a pirate of very war-like appointment gave us chase. . . .

Then, in a letter to the King:

> *To-morrow* shall I beg leave to see your kingly eyes. . . .

—the resumption of the war between them is made imminent. The scene in the graveyard thus takes place on the morrow; and this is verified for us as it ends, by the King's whisper to Laertes:

> Strengthen your patience in our *last night's* speech. . . .

The general effect produced—not, and it need not be, a very marked one—is of events moving steadily now, unhurriedly, according to plan; the deliberation of Hamlet's returning talk to the gravediggers suggests this, and it accords with the King's cold-blooded plot and Laertes' resolution.

The calendar must again be ignored after the angry parting of Hamlet and Laertes over Ophelia's grave. If it were not, Shakespeare would either have to bring in superfluous matter and most probably slacken tension (which he will certainly not want to do so near the end of his play) or explain and excuse an indecently swift passing from a funeral to a fencing match. He inserts instead a solid wedge of the history of the King's treachery and the trick played on the wretched Rosencrantz and Guildenstern. This sufficiently absorbs our attention, and dramatically separates the two incongruous events. It incidentally builds up the past still more solidly; and there is again a falsifying hint of time elapsed in Horatio's comment that

> It must be shortly known to him [Claudius] from England
> What is the issue of the business there.

—which is to be justified when all is over by the actual arrival of the English ambassadors to announce that the

> commandment is fulfilled,
> That Rosencrantz and Guildenstern are dead.

But this will simply be to give a sense of completeness to the action. Nothing is said or done to check its steady progress from the graveyard scene to the end; for that is the capital consideration involved.

It comes to this, I think. Shakespeare's true concern is with *tempo*, not time. He uses time as an auxiliary, and makes free with it, and with the calendar to make his use of it convincing.

Hamlet and the Nature of Reality

by Theodore Spencer

It is a commonplace of Shakespeare criticism that beginning with *Hamlet* and extending through the great tragedies, we are aware of an increase in scope, an enlargement of dimension, which marks a new stage in Shakespeare's dramatic career. What I should like to do in the present paper is to suggest, by an analysis of *Hamlet,* that this sense of enlargement and depth is partly brought about through an awareness of how the difference between appearance and reality could be used in the creation of dramatic character and situation. But before we come to the play itself, it will be necessary to make an apparent digression.

The average Elizabethan lived in a world very different from ours; a world in which the fundamental assumption was that of hierarchical order. There was a cosmological hierarchy, a political and social hierarchy, and a psychological hierarchy, and each was a reflection of the others. The governing of the state could be seen as an image of the order of the stars, and the order of the stars was reflected in the order of the faculties of man. The Ptolomaic heavens revolved around the earth; and as the sun was the largest and most resplendent of the planets, so the king was the center of the state. Similarly, as the earth was the center of the universe, so justice was the immovable center of political virtue. The cosmological and political orders were reflected in the order of nature: Aristotle had described it in the *De Anima* and elsewhere, and though there might be different interpretations of details, the essentials of the scheme were unhesitatingly accepted. The scale rose from inanimate matter, through the vegetative soul of plants, the sensible soul of animals, the rational soul operating through the body of man, the pure intelligence of angels, up to the pure actuality of God. Man was an essential link in the chain—the necessary mixture of body and soul to complete the order. If man did not exist, it would have been necessary—in fact it *had* been

"Hamlet and the Nature of Reality" by Theodore Spencer. From the Journal of English Literary History, V (December, 1938), 253-277. Copyright 1938 by The Johns Hopkins Press. Reprinted by permission of the publisher. This selection is from sections 2 and 3 of the essay.

necessary—to invent him. And man was more than this: he was the
end for which the rest of the universe had been created. "There is
nothing," says Raymonde de Sabonde, "in this world which does not
work day and night for man's benefit, the universe exists for him,
because of him, and was planned and arranged in its marvellous
structure for his good." [1] "This heavenly creature whom we call man,"
writes the English translator of Romei's *Courtier's Academie* (1598),
"was compounded of soule and body, the whiche body, having to be
the harbour of a most fayre and immortale soule, was created . . .
most exquisite, with his eyes toward heaven, and (man) was placed in
the midst of the world, to the end that as in an ample theatre, hee
might behold and contemplate the workes of the great God, and the
beauty of the whole world . . . and therefore man was worthily
called a little world, seeing the body of man is no other but a little
modell of the sensible world, and his soule an image of the world
intelligible." [2] Microcosm and macrocosm alike reflected the glory of
the divine architect who had planned so admirable a structure, and it
was the chief business of man on earth to study the two books—the
book of nature, and the book of the scriptures—which God had given
him, so that by knowing the truth, he could know himself, and hence
reach some knowledge of the God who had made him. The heavenly
bodies worked for man, as well as upon him: meteors and comets
foretold his future; each herb and stone had its specific virtue which
could be discovered and applied to man's benefit. "Homo est perfectio
et finis omnium creaturarum in mondo" [3]—man is the perfection and
the end of all the creatures in the world—such was the universal belief.
For he alone had reason, and though false imaginations might arouse
his passions and turn him awry, and though his humors might be un-
balanced, there was no real doubt that by the use of his distinctive
reason he could resist all such disturbances.[4] Man was not a beast, to
be the slave of his affections and his immediate experience.

So described, the system appears, as indeed it was, not only orderly
but optimistic. Yet underneath this tripartite order, of which man was
the center, there were, in the sixteenth century, certain disturbing
conceptions which painted the scene in different colors. In the first
place, the earth could be seen, according to the Ptolomaic system, not
only as the center and most important part of the universe, but as
exactly the opposite. It could be regarded, to use Professor Lovejoy's
words, as "the place farthest removed from the Empyrean, the bottom

[1] I translate from Montaigne's translation of the *Natural Theology*, Chapter 97.
[2] Translated by I. K., London, 1598, pp. 16-17.
[3] Motto on a diagram in R. Fludd, *Philosophia Sacra*, etc., Frankfurt, 1626.
[4] This point is well brought out by Hardin Craig, "Shakespeare's Depiction of
Passions," *Philological Quarterly*, 10 (1925), 289-301.

of the creation, to which its dregs and baser elements sank." [5] Or, as
Marston put it, in more Elizabethan language: "This earth is the only
grave and Golgotha wherein all things that live must rot; 'tis but the
draught wherein the heavenly bodies discharge their corruption; the
very muckhill on which the sublunary orbs cast their excrements." [6]
In the second place, man, the chief inhabitant of this tiny and remote
globe, could be regarded as equally unworthy and corrupt, for since
the fall of Adam he had only a faint glimmering of its original gift
of natural reason, and hence, through his own fault, he was the only
creature who had disrupted the system. The miseries of man, as a
consequence of this fact, were very heavily emphasized in the sixteenth century by moralists and satirists alike. The introduction to
the seventh book of Pliny's *Natural History,* in which the wretchedness of the human situation, compared with that of animals, is described at length, was adapted and re-emphasized again and again: in
1570 Gascoigne enthusiastically translated Pope Innocent III's *De Contemptu Mundi;* the keynote of Marston's Cynic Satire (*Scourge of
Villainy,* 1598, No. 7)—as of Marston's view of man in general—is that
while all the other orders of nature fulfill their proper function, man
alone has lost his specific virtue:

> And now no humane creatures, once disrai'd
> Of that faire iem.
> Beasts *sence,* plants *growth,* like being as a stone,
> But out alas, our Cognisance is gone.

A thousand similar illustrations could be given from sixteenth century literature, and I believe that if they were arranged in chrono-
logical order they would show an increase both in frequency and
intensity as the century approached its end, for there was a firm conviction in the minds of many people of the time that no age was so
corrupt as their own. In fact, it was so bad that probably the last judgment was not far off.

Thus, in the inherited, the universally accepted, Christian view of
man and his universe there was an implicit conflict between man's
dignity and wretchedness: a conflict which was also a complement.
For instance, Pierre Boaystuau, in 1557 (the work was translated into
English in 1603), wrote a treatise called *Le Theatre du Monde, ou
il est faict un ample discours des misères humaines,* which is immediately followed, bound in the same volume, by *"un brief discours
sur l'excellence et dignité de l'homme."* The two views existed side

[5] A. O. Lovejoy, *The Great Chain of Being,* Cambridge, Massachusetts, 1936, pp.
101-102. In my opinion, Mr. Lovejoy here exaggerates the prevalence of this more
pessimistic view. The other was equally common—probably more so.
[6] *The Malcontent,* IV. ii.

by side, and a writer could choose which one he pleased, according to his temperament, the state of his feelings, or his hortatory intention.

This particular conflict, however, no matter how deep it went and no matter how many aspects it presented, could after all be solved; the doctrines of grace and redemption existed for the purpose. But there was another conflict, more particular to the sixteenth century, and, since it was new, perhaps more emotionally and intellectually disturbing. It consisted in this: that in the sixteenth century each one of the interrelated orders—cosmological, political, and natural—which were the frame, the basic pattern, of all Elizabethan thinking, was being punctured by a doubt. Copernicus had questioned the cosmological order, Machiavelli had questioned the political order, Montaigne had questioned the natural order. The consequences were enormous.

In order to understand what the theory of Copernicus implied, it is necessary to have as vivid a picture as possible of the difference between his system and the Aristotelian or Ptolomaic. Upon the structure of the Ptolomaic system, with the earth in the center, everything had been built: the order of creation, astrology, the theory of the microcosm and the macrocosm, the parallels between the universe and the state. But when the sun was put at the center, and the earth set between Mars and Venus as a mobile and subsidiary planet, the whole elaborate structure, with all its interdependencies, so easy to visualize, so convenient for metaphor and allusion, lost its meaning. "If the celestial spheres," said Hooker, "should forget their wonted motions, and by irregular volubility turn themselves any way . . . what would become of man himself, whom all these things do now serve?" [7]

We must, however, as Miss Marjorie Nicolson and others have shown, be on our guard against over-emphasizing the effects of the Copernican theory on the popular mind. It was confronted at first, considering its implications, with remarkably little opposition. For though Luther and Melancthon attacked his views (they contradicted certain phrases of Scripture), and Copernicus' book was published by the cautious Osiander with an apologetic preface and the word "hypothesis" on the title page, no official steps were taken against it until 1616, when, because Galileo supported it, it was finally put on the Index. Even then the censure was mild: anyone could read it if nine sentences were changed so that they were turned from statements of fact into matters of conjecture.

The reason for this mildness has been made clear by Mr. Francis Johnson and other historians of sixteenth century science. For the Copernican system could be looked at in two ways: as a mathematical

[7] Quoted by J. B. Black, *The Reign of Elizabeth,* Oxford, 1936, p. 261.

theory and as a description of physical fact. Being simpler than the elaborate Ptolomaic system, it was welcomed by mathematicians as an easier means of making astronomical calculations, but it was not until Galileo perfected the telescope that it was seriously considered to be a true description of reality. Even Galileo at first hesitated to support it, not because he feared it would get him into trouble, but because he feared it might make him ridiculous. Nothing could show more clearly how strongly the Ptolomaic view was entrenched.

And naturally so. For the whole inherited order depended on it, as Donne was one of the first people to realize. He saw—the lines from the *First Anniversary* are almost too familiar to quote—that the new astronomy not only set the inherited cosmology awry, so that the sun and the earth were lost, it also affected the state, the order of society, and the individual:

> Prince, subject, father, son, are things forgot
> For every man alone thinks he hath got
> To be a phoenix, and that then can be
> None of that kind of which he is, but he.

It broke down the order which Ulysses, in Shakespeare's *Troilus and Cressida* (I, ii) had so admirably expounded, and which so intimately related to each other the planets, the government of states, and the government of the individual. In considering its effects one can almost sympathize with the Jesuit who, two hundred years later, taught the young Stendhal the Ptolomaic system, "because it explained everything and was supported by the Church."

The ideas of Machiavelli had a different reception from those of Copernicus. Though for about half a generation after *The Prince* was published its views attracted no very remarkable degree of attention, once they were seriously considered the storm broke with what now seems an extraordinary violence. No term of abuse was too strong for Machiavelli's principles, works, and character. The Jesuits of Ingolstadt burned him in effigy; to Cardinal Pole he was obviously inspired by the devil; he was put on the Index as soon as that institution was founded; the protestants considered his ideas directly responsible for the massacre of St. Bartholomew. He was universally described as an atheist and an unscrupulous fiend; he became, in Signor Praz's words, "a rallying point for whatever was most loathsome in statecraft, and indeed in human nature at large." [8]

The reasons for Machiavelli's reputation can perhaps best be realized by comparing *The Prince* with the *De Officiis* of Cicero, just as

---

[8] Mario Praz, "Machiavelli and the Elizabethans," *Proceedings of the British Academy*, 13 (1928), 8.

the effect of the Copernican system can best be seen by comparing it
with the Ptolomaic. For the *De Officiis,* as much as the *Politics* of
Aristotle, from which it was partly derived, represents the official
sixteenth century doctrine. Prudence, justice, liberality, greatness of
soul, these and other virtues characterized the public man; the life of
reason, in public as in private, implied the pursuit of virtue. All
medieval thought said the same thing; it was the basis of political
theory, and like the inherited Elizabethan psychology, it was fundamentally optimistic, and it was intimately concerned with morality.
But Machiavelli, in the words of J. W. Allen, "thought of the state
as a morally isolated thing." [9] He was fundamentally practical. He
regarded human history divorced from revelation, and human nature
divorced from grace; he looked at man, as Bacon said, not as he should
be, but as he is, and he found that man was naturally evil and that the
best way to govern him for his own good was by fear and by force.
The view may have been sound, but it was outrageous to Elizabethan
sensibilities. Was this the truth, underneath the idealistic appearance,
about man as a political animal? The Elizabethans refused to believe
it: the violence of their feeling on the subject may be taken as an
indication that, below the surface, they realized—with a half-horrified
fascination—that the ideas of Machiavelli, which they received in so
distorted a form, might after all be true.

Montaigne's position is less easy to summarize. But the implication
of his ideas, at least those in the *Apology for Raymond Sebonde,*
could be just as devastating to the inherited view of man's place in
the natural sphere as the ideas of Copernicus and Machiavelli might
be to man's place in the spheres of cosmology and politics. Again
this is brought out most clearly by contrast, and this time we need
go no further than the work which Montaigne was apparently setting
out to defend. I know of no book which more optimistically and
thoroughly describes the inherited view of the order of nature than
Sabonde's *Natural Theology.* Its optimism is, in fact, almost heretical.
All the ranks of nature, he says, lead up to man: his reason sets him
apart from all the other animals, and by a proper use of it he can
come to a full knowledge of himself, the external world, and God.

But these are just the assumptions that Montaigne, in his *Apology,*
sets out to deny. Man can know nothing by himself, says Montaigne;
he cannot know God, he cannot know his soul, he cannot know nature. His senses are hopelessly unreliable, there are no satisfactory
standards of beauty or of anything else, everything is in a flux, and
the only way man can rise from his ignorant and ignominious position
is by divine assistance. His purpose in writing the essay, says Mon-

[9] J. W. Allen, *History of Political Thought in the Sixteenth Century,* New York,
1928, p. 477.

taigne, is to make people "sensible of the inanity, the vanity, and in-
significance of man; to wrest out of their fists the miserable weapon
of their reason; to make them bow the head and bite the dust under
the authority and reverence of the divine majesty." [10]

Of course all this, though extreme, is neither entirely unorthodox
nor necessarily disturbing. From one point of view, it is related to
what Innocent III said in the *De Contemptu Mundi,* and what count-
less other reputable writers had said before and since. But there was
one point—and it was this that bothered the authorities in Rome
(from their point of view quite rightly), when they examined the
Essais in 1582—which was *not* orthodox and which *was* disturbing.
Montaigne gave the appearance of saying that there was no fundamental difference between the faculties of man and those of animals.
His remarks, to be sure, are highly ambiguous, probably on purpose,
but he suggests that animals have the capacity, hitherto and for
obvious reasons attributed to man alone, of abstracting from sensible
phenomena their essential characteristics, and of making them con-
form, to use his own words, to the soul's "immortal and spiritual
condition." [11] Such a statement has wide implications; it implies, as
Montaigne's whole argument, of which this passage is the climax,
tends to imply, that there are no true distinctions between the psychology of man and the psychology of animals; that reason amounts
to nothing, and that in consequence the whole hierarchy of nature,
at a crucial point, is destroyed.

I hope I have made it clear, through these introductory remarks,
that the idea of man which lay behind Shakespearean tragedy was, in
the first place, inextricably interwoven with the ideas of the state and
the world as a whole to a degree which it is difficult for us to realize,
and, in the second place, that this interwoven pattern was threatened
by an implicit and an explicit conflict. At the time when Shakespeare
wrote *Hamlet* there were available for emotional contemplation and
for dramatic representation two views of man's nature, two views of
the world, two views of the state. Drama could be not merely the
conflict between romantic love and external forces, as in *Romeo and
Juliet;* it could represent a conflict far more complicated and far more
profound.

It would be a fascinating and rewarding study to analyze in detail
just why this conflict seemed particularly alive at this particular moment. The pressure of material forces, social and economic, the political and religious situation, the growth of a realistic and satiric school
of literature, the recrudescence of an emphasis on death—all these

[10] *Essays,* 2, 12, translated by E. J. Trechmann, Oxford, 1927, 1, 439-440.
[11] *Essays,* ed. cit. 1, 475.

things, as well as others, contributed to a movement, emotional rather than intellectual, which from one point of view might be described as the Counter-Renaissance. But a treatment of this, however necessary, must be reserved for another occasion. Our present business is with the text of *Hamlet* itself. I hope to show that an awareness of the difference between appearance and reality, based on the fact that there was a deep conflict in the contemporary views of man and his world, is woven into the texture of the play, and is largely responsible for the enormous increase in size which characterizes *Hamlet* over any of its predecessors. Not that Shakespeare deliberately reflects the Copernican system, or the ideas of Machiavelli or Montaigne: to say that would be nonsense. The split they illustrate was merely a part of Shakespeare's emotional climate; many sensitive minds were aware of it; he alone turned it to full dramatic use. The creation of dramatic suspense by an internal conflict in a mind aware of the evil reality under the good appearance is the core of the greatness, the originality of *Hamlet*.

We may best begin our discussion by observing what sort of man Hamlet was before his mother's second marriage. According to Ophelia he had a "noble mind," "the courtier's, soldier's, scholar's, eye, tongue, sword." He was

> The expectancy and rose of the fair state,
> The glass of fashion and the mould of form,

a man with a "noble and most sovereign reason." In other words, he was an ideal Renaissance nobleman, himself an idealist, with—to use Bradley's somewhat romantic expression—"an unbounded delight and faith in everything good and beautiful."

But the discovery of his mother's lust and the fact that the kingdom is in the hands of an unworthy man (Hamlet's—the prince's—feeling that the king is not worthy of his position is a more important part of his state of mind when the play opens than is usually realized)—these facts shatter his picture of the world, the state, and the individual. His sense of the evil in all three spheres is as closely interwoven in his first soliloquy as all three spheres were interwoven in sixteenth century thought. It is characteristic of Shakespeare's conception of Hamlet's universalizing mind that he should make Hamlet think, first, of the general rottenness: to him all the uses of the world are weary, stale, flat, and unprofitable, and things rank and gross in nature possess it entirely. From this he passes to a consideration of the excellence of his father as king, compared to his satyr-like uncle, and he finally dwells at length on the lustfulness of his mother, who has violated the natural law by the brevity of her grief and the hastiness of her marriage.

> O God! a beast, that wants discourse of reason,
> Would have mourned longer.

In other words, in first presenting Hamlet to his audience, Shakespeare uses an interwoven series of references to the world, the state, and the individual, and one reason this first soliloquy is so broken, its rhythms so panting, is that it reflects Hamlet's disillusionment about all three spheres at once. So closely were they related in contemporary thought that to smash one was to smash the others as well.

This, of course, is not the only place where Hamlet thinks in general terms: one of his most striking habits is to stretch his thought to embrace the world as a whole, to talk of infinite space, to use rhetoric that includes the stars. For example, it is characteristic of him that when he approaches Laertes after Laertes has jumped into Ophelia's grave, he should ask who it is who

> Conjures the wandering stars, and makes them stand
> Like wonder-wounded hearers,

when, as a matter of fact, Laertes had not mentioned the stars at all. It is as if Hamlet were attributing to Laertes a thought that would be natural to him, but not to Laertes. Again, the first thing that Hamlet exclaims after the ghost has given his message is "O all you host of heaven!"; and, in his mother's closet, when he upbraids her with her marriage, he describes it not merely as violating human contracts, but as affecting the world as a whole:

> heaven's face doth glow,
> Yea this solidity and compound mass,
> With tristful visage, as against the doom,
> Is thought-sick at the act.

But the occasion on which Hamlet speaks at greatest length of the heavens is, of course, when he describes his state of mind to Rosencrantz and Guildenstern in the second act. It is perhaps worth while, before quoting the passage, to remind ourselves again of the orthodox description of the beauty of the heavens—the heavens of which Spenser had so glowingly written in his "Hymn of Heavenly Beautie," and which Thomas Digges in his "Perfit Description of the Coelestiall Orbes" (1576) describes more scientifically, but with equal enthusiasm. Digges is referring to the motionless heaven of fixed stars according to the Copernican system, and in his case, as in others, the acceptance of Copernicus did not mean that the universe was not beautiful. "This orbe of starres," he says, "fixed infinitely up extendeth himself in altitude sphericallye and therefore immovable the palace of foelicitie garnished with perpetually shininge glorious lightes

innumerable, farr excellinge our sonne both in quantitye and quali-
tye, the very courte of coellestiall angelles devoid of griefe and re-
plenished with perfite endlesse ioye the habitacle for the elect." [12]
Perhaps Shakespeare was even thinking of this description: Digges
was a kind of sixteenth century Eddington or Jeans; his book went
through six editions before 1600; Shakespeare could have found these
words merely by looking at the title page, where they are inscribed in
a diagram; and Hamlet's description of the heaven sounds more like
the motionless outer sphere of Copernicus than the revolving heaven
of Ptolemy. Be that as it may, what Shakespeare does is to use the
traditional feeling about the heavens as a background to bring out an
important side of Hamlet's character; nothing could show better the
largeness of Hamlet's mind and his present melancholy; for he sees
in the heavens, as well as in his own situation, the reality of evil underneath the appearance of good. To understand the force of his
remarks we should have clearly in our minds the thousand and one
sixteenth century repetitions of the old teaching, with which every
member of Shakespeare's audience must have been familiar, that the
surest way to understand man's place in the world and to realize the
magnificence of God's creation, was to contemplate the glory of the
superior heavens which surrounded the earth. But what Hamlet says
is exactly the opposite.

> This most excellent canopy the air, look you, this brave o'erhanging
> firmament, this majestical roof fretted with golden fire, why, it ap-
> peareth nothing to me but a foul and pestilent congregation of vapors.

And from this consideration of the macrocosm he passes at once to the
microcosm: the sequence of thought was, in his time, almost inevitable; and again he uses the familiar vocabulary of his age (I follow the
punctuation of the second quarto and of Dover Wilson, which alone
makes sense in terms of Elizabethan psychology):

> What a piece of work is a man, how noble in reason, how infinite in
> faculties, in form and moving, how express and admirable in action,
> how like an angel in apprehension, how like a god: the beauty of the
> world; the paragon of animals; and yet to me, what is this quintessence
> of dust? Man delights not me.

This use of generalization, which is one of the most attractive and
important sides to Hamlet's character, illustrates more than Shakespeare's way of describing a single individual; it also illustrates a

[12] See Francis R. Johnson, *Astronomical Thought in Renaissance England*, Balti-
more, 1937, p. 166. Digges' tract is published in *The Huntington Library Bulletin*,
No. 5, April, 1934, by F. R. Johnson and S. V. Larkey.

dramatic device which Shakespeare frequently used at this period in his career, the device of weaving into the texture of his play a point of view or standard of values which the action is violating, but against which—for the proper understanding of the play—the action must be seen. The two great speeches of Ulysses in *Troilus and Cressida* are perhaps the best illustration of this device, but *Hamlet* itself is full of examples. Hamlet's own remarks about reason, the specific virtue of a human being (which Montaigne had so ingeniously labored to minimize) are a case in point. Horatio speaks (I.iv.73) of the "sovereignty of reason," as does Ophelia, but Hamlet, as is eminently appropriate in a play where the conflict is so much inside a man, is the one who describes the traditional view most fully (IV.iv.33):

> What is a man,
> If his chief good and market of his time
> Be but to sleep and feed? a beast, no more.
> Sure he that made us with such large discourse,
> Looking before and after, gave us not
> That capability and god-like reason
> To fust in us unus'd.

It is worth observing in what terms Shakespeare speaks of reason in the important passages throughout the play. Reason, the specific function of man in the order of nature, is twice referred to as "noble," an adjective, like "sovereign" (also applied to reason), that has connotations in the political order, and, in the passage I have just quoted, it is described as "god-like," an adjective that, to an Elizabethan would have cosmological connotations as well. It may not be fantastic to see, in this adjectival microcosm, an image of the macrocosm I have been trying to define.

At all events, the standard which Hamlet's soliloquy describes is not only the standard which his own behavior violates; it is also the standard which was violated by Gertrude in mourning so briefly for her first husband, and in unnaturally yielding to her lust, so that her reason, in Hamlet's words, has become a pandar to her will, her fleshly desire. In both cases, the appearance, the accepted natural order of good and of the supremacy of reason, is destroyed by the individual reality of evil, and man has sunk to the level of animals, his specific function gone.

The New Doubt

by D. G. James

My own wish is frankly to elevate Hamlet's intellectual distresses to an equality in importance with his emotional state; the strength of the emotional shock he has suffered is equalled by the weakness of his mind in the face of difficult moral and metaphysical issues. Hamlet was, after all, an intellectual. We must bear in mind that Shakespeare was the first to make him a member of a university; and *Hamlet* was acted before the universities of Oxford and Cambridge. (We may also recall, with alarm, that Polonius had been a member of a university; some will further note, and with still greater alarm, that he had clearly, when at the university, been a member of the Dramatic Society.) But my point is that *Hamlet* is not a tragedy of excessive thought; so far as we are to see the cause of Hamlet's destiny in intellectual terms, it is a tragedy not of excessive thought but of defeated thought. Hamlet does not know; and he knows of no way of knowing. And then comes the line,

> Thus conscience does make cowards of us all;

resolution is sicklied o'er, and enterprise loses the name of action. It is hard to know what it is right to do; and we do not know whether in fact we live after we die, and in a universe in which a moral order asserts itself. No doubt Shakespeare had to be careful how he expressed the issues which confronted Hamlet. But the plain issue was, Does God exist or not? What was at stake in Hamlet's mind was nothing less than the greatest which confronts our mortal minds.

"Conscience does make cowards of us." There has been, I am aware, much dispute as to what the word means here. For my part, I find not the least difficulty in believing that the word carries both its usual meaning and that of "reflection and anxious thought." It is a platitude of Shakespeare study that Shakespeare could, with wonderful ease, charge a word with two or three meanings at once; there is hardly a page of Shakespeare which does not illustrate this; and, in any case, the word "conscience" means for us all both a command to do what is right and anxious reflection as to what is, in fact, the right thing to do. If I had to choose (what I feel under no compulsion whatever to do) between the two meanings proposed, I should unhesitatingly choose the former and usual meaning. A. C. Bradley was cross (in a footnote) with the *Oxford Dictionary* for giving its authority to construing "conscience" in this passage as meaning "moral sense or scrupulousness"; and he declares that "in this soliloquy Hamlet is not thinking of the duty laid upon him at all." But how then can he begin to explain the lines,

> Whether 'tis nobler in the mind to suffer . . .
> Or to take arms . . . ?

It is precisely his duty Hamlet thinks of, and of his duty, which he finds it hard to decide, in relation to a possible world to come; and the difficulty of knowing what is right, and the uncertainty of our last destiny, together puzzle and arrest the will. Conscience requires that we do what is right; but then, what *is* right or wrong in these circumstances? Anxious reflection discloses no clear conviction; nor does it provide knowledge of a world to come. This is the moral and metaphysical uncertainty in which Hamlet finds himself. He does not know and cannot find out. Conscience makes demands; but it also provides no clear moral or metaphysical sense. Until he finds himself in this climacteric condition, life has gone on smoothly enough; but now, and suddenly, he knows that he lacks the insight, or the knowledge, or the faith, which will steady him, and carry him forward in a single and continuous course of action. In this, Hamlet knows he is different from Horatio, whose calm and steadily appointed way of life we are expected to admire. Horatio is precisely one who in suffering all, suffers nothing; he has accepted the first alternative Hamlet had proposed to himself: "whether 'tis nobler in the mind to suffer the slings and arrows . . ." Horatio has, we are expected to understand, decided that it is nobler so to suffer, and he has taken the buffets and the rewards of fortune with equal thanks; he knows his line and he is steady in it. Hamlet has not decided; and hence his peculiar distress.

It is very important to observe the play here on the word "suffer." Horatio is one who suffers everything and suffers nothing. What does this mean? I take it to mean, in the first sense, that Horatio accepts equally the fortunes and misfortunes of life; he embraces his good fortune with restraint and he endures his misfortunes. Therefore, in the second sense, he suffers nothing; he is not put out or mastered by circumstance; he is master of himself and of circumstance; he sustains a steady and imperturbable calm. In the one sense of the word, he takes what comes, without rebellion against it; he does not oppose it to end it; he is thus passive. But in the other sense, he is precisely not passive, but pre-eminently active and creative in his life. Such a steadiness and even tenor, in a philosophy of "suffering," Hamlet does not possess. Horatio is one who, in suffering all, suffers nothing; Hamlet is one who, in suffering nothing, suffers everything. He is active where Horatio is passive, and passive where Horatio is active. His passivity is of the wrong sort; he is blown about by every gust of passion. But it is the same when he is active: his activity, like his passivity, is an affair of passion merely. Judgment is not in it. He is passion's slave, played on like a pipe, lapsed in time and circumstance, unaccountable, now listless, now violent.

But we must remark how Hamlet speaks of Horatio; he does so in words of passionate admiration. His election had sealed Horatio for himself because in suffering all, Horatio suffered nothing; and it is the man who is not passion's slave whom he would wear in his heart's core. How clearly he would be like Horatio! And yet, in the face of what has happened, ought he to be like Horatio? or ought he not to take up arms against his troubles, and violently end them and perhaps thereby himself? He did not know. The ghost had given Hamlet specific instructions to contrive nothing against his mother:

> . . . leave her to heaven,
> And to those thorns that in her bosom lodge,
> To prick and sting her.

But ought he perhaps to leave Claudius to heaven also? When his guilt was proved beyond any doubt, Hamlet still did not kill him; he left him alone, giving a reason, plausible enough in Hamlet's eyes, in the eyes of his audience, and in our eyes, and yet inhabiting a middle region between sincerity and insincerity. We are told that in explaining why he does not there kill the King, Hamlet was sincere; it was a belief of the time. But it was certainly not universal. Claudius at least could have told him it was nonsense; Claudius has made just clear to us what was necessary if he, Claudius, was to win heaven. And could a Hamlet who half his time believed neither in heaven nor hell, sincerely and with a whole mind say these things? He leaves Claudius, and goes off to rage at his mother.

Conscience, says Hamlet, makes cowards of us; we are made afraid by it; and who of us does not know that this is true? In the soliloquy in Act IV (How all occasions do inform against me) the same thought is uppermost. God has given us capability and god-like reason; we may, Hamlet certainly does not, live in a bestial oblivion of it. What he charges himself with is excess of scruple in employing it in his moral difficulties, thinking too precisely on the event; his scruples, he says, are craven; or at least they are one part wisdom and three quarters cowardice:

> A thought which, quarter'd, hath but one part wisdom
> And ever three parts coward.

He is disposed to upbraid himself for letting all things sleep; but he also acknowledges, even in his bitter reproachment of himself, that he is at least one-quarter wise in thinking precisely on the event: he could not do other than think precisely on such momentous issues. But then, if his precise thinking issues in no results, no assured decision, no clear path of duty, how can he be other than afraid of doing one thing rather than the other? He has cause and will and strength and means to do it; yes, all these he has; but has he the conscience to do it? That is the question; and conscience makes cowards of us. But where is a resolution of this distress to come from? From thinking precisely on the event? Apparently not; Hamlet is a thinker and has thought enough. Then let him plunge, and do what no doubt most people would expect of him; he talks fustian at himself about greatly finding quarrel in a straw when honor's at the stake; and this in future will be his line. But will it? Of course not. It is better to have three quarters cowardice and one quarter wisdom than four quarters of bravado and tomfoolery; and Hamlet knows this well enough. But where and how will he find escape from this proper and rightminded cowardice? This is his problem; and it is, I suppose, everybody's problem.

I am aware that I may well be manifesting a deplorable cocksureness in all this. But at least I shall make clear what I intend; and I confess to some impatience with what seems to me the present-day willingness to give up Hamlet for a mystery. Now it is true, no doubt, that we must not see the play as merely an affair of the character of its hero. But few of us will deny that Hamlet's procrastination is the major fact in the play and that it was intended by Shakespeare to be so. But are we really to find his procrastination a mystery and to leave it a mystery? Is there really anything mysterious about a man who has come to no clear and practiced sense of life, and who in the face of a shocking situation which quite peculiarly involves him, shuffles, deceives himself, procrastinates, and in his exasperation cruelly persecutes the person he loves best in the world? Is this beyond our understanding? If we fail to understand it, is it not only because it is all so near to us and not because it is far off in Elizabethan times? Conscience, Hamlet said, makes cowards *of us all.* He was thinking of himself not as the exception, but as the rule.

The World of *Hamlet*

by *Maynard Mack*

My subject is the world of *Hamlet*. I do not of course mean Denmark, except as Denmark is given a body by the play; and I do not mean Elizabethan England, though this is necessarily close behind the scenes. I mean simply the imaginative environment that the play asks us to enter when we read it or go to see it.

Great plays, as we know, do present us with something that can be called a world, a microcosm—a world like our own in being made of people, actions, situations, thoughts, feelings, and much more, but unlike our own in being perfectly, or almost perfectly, significant and coherent. In a play's world, each part implies the other parts, and each lives, each means, with the life and meaning of the rest.

This is the reason, as we also know, that the worlds of great plays greatly differ. Othello in Hamlet's position, we sometimes say, would have no problem; but what we are really saying is that Othello in Hamlet's position would not exist. The conception we have of Othello is a function of the characters who help define him, Desdemona, honest Iago, Cassio, and the rest; of his history of travel and war; of a great storm that divides his ship from Cassio's, and a handkerchief; of a quiet night in Venice broken by cries about an old black ram; of a quiet night in Cyprus broken by swordplay; of a quiet bedroom where a woman goes to bed in her wedding sheets and a man comes in with a light to put out the light; and above all, of a language, a language with many voices in it, gentle, rasping, querulous, or foul, but all counterpointing the one great voice:

> Put up your bright swords, for the dew will rust them.
>
> O thou weed
> Who art so lovely fair and smell'st so sweet
> That the sense aches at thee. . . .
>
> Yet I'll not shed her blood
> Nor scar that whiter skin of hers than snow,
> And smooth as monumental alabaster.

"The World of Hamlet*" by Maynard Mack. From* The Yale Review, *XLI (1952), 502-523. Copyright © 1952 by the Yale University Press. Reprinted by permission of the author and the publisher.*

I pray you in your letters,
When you shall these unlucky deeds relate,
Speak of me as I am; nothing extenuate,
Nor set down aught in malice; then must you speak
Of one that loved not wisely but too well;
Of one not easily jealous, but being wrought,
Perplex'd in th' extreme; of one whose hand,
Like the base Indian, threw a pearl away
Richer than all his tribe. . . .

Without his particular world of voices, persons, events, the world that both expresses and contains him, Othello is unimaginable. And so, I think, are Antony, King Lear, Macbeth—and Hamlet. We come back then to Hamlet's world, of all the tragic worlds that Shakespeare made, easily the most various and brilliant, the most elusive. It is with no thought of doing justice to it that I have singled out three of its attributes for comment. I know too well, if I may echo a sentiment of Mr. E. M. W. Tillyard's, that no one is likely to accept another man's reading of *Hamlet,* that anyone who tries to throw light on one part of the play usually throws the rest into deeper shadow, and that what I have to say leaves out many problems—to mention only one, the knotty problem of the text. All I would say in defense of the materials I have chosen is that they seem to me interesting, close to the root of the matter even if we continue to differ about what the root of the matter is, and explanatory, in a modest way, of this play's peculiar hold on everyone's imagination, its almost mythic status, one might say, as a paradigm of the life of man.

The first attribute that impresses us, I think, is mysteriousness. We often hear it said, perhaps with truth, that every great work of art has a mystery at the heart; but the mystery of *Hamlet* is something else. We feel its presence in the numberless explanations that have been brought forward for Hamlet's delay, his madness, his ghost, his treatment of Polonius, or Ophelia, or his mother; and in the controversies that still go on about whether the play is "undoubtedly a failure" (Eliot's phrase) or one of the greatest artistic triumphs; whether, if it is a triumph, it belongs to the highest order of tragedy; whether, if it is such a tragedy, its hero is to be taken as a man of exquisite moral sensibility (Bradley's view) or an egomaniac (Madariaga's view).

Doubtless there have been more of these controversies and explanations than the play requires; for in Hamlet, to paraphrase a remark of Falstaff's, we have a character who is not only mad in himself but a cause that madness is in the rest of us. Still, the very existence of so many theories and counter-theories, many of them formulated by sober heads, gives food for thought. *Hamlet* seems to lie closer to the illogical logic of life than Shakespeare's other tragedies. And while the causes of this situation may be sought by saying that Shakespeare revised the play so often that eventually the motivations were smudged over, or that the original old play has been here or there imperfectly digested, or that the problems of Hamlet lay so close to Shakespeare's heart that he could not quite distance them in the formal terms of art, we have still as critics to deal with effects, not causes. If I may quote again from Mr. Tillyard, the play's very lack of a rigorous type of causal logic seems to be a part of its point.

Moreover, the matter goes deeper than this. Hamlet's world is pre-eminently in the interrogative mood. It reverberates with questions, anguished, meditative, alarmed. There are questions that in this play, to an extent I think unparalleled in any other, mark the phases and even the nuances of the action, helping to establish its peculiar baffled tone. There are other questions whose interrogations, innocent at first glance, are subsequently seen to have reached beyond their contexts and to point towards some pervasive inscrutability in Hamlet's world as a whole. Such is that tense series of challenges with which the tragedy begins: Bernardo's of Francisco, "Who's there?" Francisco's of Horatio and Marcellus, "Who is there?" Horatio's of the ghost, "What art thou . . . ?" And then there are the famous questions. In them the interrogations seem to point not only beyond the context but beyond the play, out of Hamlet's predicaments into everyone's: "What a piece of work is a man! . . . And yet to me what is this quintessence of dust?" "To be, or not to be, that is the question." "Get thee to a nunnery. Why wouldst thou be a breeder of sinners?" "I am very proud, revengeful, ambitious, with more offences at my beck than I have thoughts to put them in, imagination to give them shape, or time to act them in. What should such fellows as I do crawling between earth and heaven?" "Dost thou think Alexander look'd o' this fashion i' th' earth? . . . And smelt so?"

Further, Hamlet's world is a world of riddles. The hero's own language is often riddling, as the critics have pointed out. When he puns, his puns have receding depths in them, like the one which constitutes his first speech: "A little more than kin, and less than kind." His utterances in madness, even if wild and whirling, are simultaneously, as Polonius discovers, pregnant: "Do you know me, my lord?" "Excellent well. You are a fishmonger." Even the madness itself is riddling: How much is real? How much is feigned? What does it mean? Sane or mad, Hamlet's mind plays restlessly about his world, turning up one riddle upon another. The riddle of character, for example, and how it is that in a man whose virtues

else are "pure as grace," some vicious mole of nature, some "dram
of eale," can "all the noble substance oft adulter." Or the riddle
of the player's art, and how a man can so project himself into a fiction, a dream of passion, that he can weep for Hecuba. Or the
riddle of action: how we may think too little—"What to ourselves
in passion we propose," says the player-king, "The passion ending,
doth the purpose lose;" and again, how we may think too much:
"Thus conscience does make cowards of us all, And thus the native
hue of resolution Is sicklied o'er with the pale cast of thought."

There are also more immediate riddles. His mother—how could
she "on this fair mountain leave to feed, And batten on this moor?"
The ghost—which may be a devil, for "the de'il hath power T'
assume a pleasing shape." Ophelia—what does her behavior to him
mean? Surprising her in her closet, he falls to such perusal of her
face as he would draw it. Even the king at his prayers is a riddle.
Will a revenge that takes him in the purging of his soul be vengeance, or hire and salary? As for himself, Hamlet realizes, he is
the greatest riddle of all—a mystery, he warns Rosencrantz and
Guildenstern, from which he will not have the heart plucked out.
He cannot tell why he has of late lost all his mirth, forgone all
custom of exercises. Still less can he tell why he delays: "I do not
know Why yet I live to say, 'This thing's to do,' Sith I have cause
and will and strength and means To do 't."

Thus the mysteriousness of Hamlet's world is of a piece. It
is not simply a matter of missing motivations, to be expunged if
only we could find the perfect clue. It is built in. It is evidently
an important part of what the play wishes to say to us. And it is
certainly an element that the play thrusts upon us from the opening
word. Everyone, I think, recalls the mysteriousness of that first scene.
The cold middle of the night on the castle platform, the muffled
sentries, the uneasy atmosphere of apprehension, the challenges
leaping out of the dark, the questions that follow the challenges,
feeling out the darkness, searching for identities, for relations, for
assurance. "Bernardo?" "Have you had quiet guard?" "Who hath
reliev'd you?" "What, is Horatio there?" "What, has this thing
appear'd again tonight?" "Looks 'a not like the king?" "How now,
Horatio! . . . Is not this something more than fantasy? What think
you on 't?" "It is not like the king?" "Why this same strict and most
observant watch . . . ?" "Shall I strike at it with my partisan?" "Do
you consent we shall acquaint [young Hamlet] with it?"

We need not be surprised that critics and playgoers alike have
been tempted to see in this an evocation not simply of Hamlet's
world but of their own. Man in his aspect of bafflement, moving
in darkness on a rampart between two worlds, unable to reject,
or quite accept, the one that, when he faces it, "to-shakes" his dis-

position with thoughts beyond the reaches of his soul—comforting himself with hints and guesses. We hear these hints and guesses whispering through the darkness as the several watchers speak. "At least, the whisper goes so," says one. "I think it be no other but e'en so," says another. "I have heard" that on the crowing of the cock "Th' extravagant and erring spirit hies To his confine," says a third. "Some say" at Christmas time "this bird of dawning" sings all night, "And then, they say, no spirit dare stir abroad." "So have I heard," says the first, "and do in part believe it." However we choose to take the scene, it is clear that it creates a world where uncertainties are of the essence.

Meantime, such is Shakespeare's economy, a second attribute of Hamlet's world has been put before us. This is the problematic nature of reality and the relation of reality to appearance. The play begins with an appearance, an "apparition," to use Marcellus's term—the ghost. And the ghost is somehow real, indeed the vehicle of realities. Through its revelation, the glittering surface of Claudius's court is pierced, and Hamlet comes to know, and we do, that the king is not only hateful to him but the murderer of his father, that his mother is guilty of adultery as well as incest. Yet there is a dilemma in the revelation. For possibly the apparition *is* an apparition, a devil who has assumed his father's shape.

This dilemma, once established, recurs on every hand. From the court's point of view, there is Hamlet's madness. Polonius investigates and gets some strange advice about his daughter: "Conception is a blessing, but as your daughter may conceive, friend, look to 't." Rosencrantz and Guildenstern investigate and get the strange confidence that "Man delights not me; no, nor woman neither." Ophelia is "loosed" to Hamlet (Polonius's vulgar word), while Polonius and the king hide behind the arras; and what they hear is a strange indictment of human nature, and a riddling threat: "Those that are married already, all but one, shall live."

On the other hand, from Hamlet's point of view, there is Ophelia. Kneeling here at her prayers, she seems the image of innocence and devotion. Yet she is of the sex for whom he has already found the name Frailty, and she is also, as he seems either madly or sanely to divine, a decoy in a trick. The famous cry—"Get thee to a nunnery"—shows the anguish of his uncertainty. If Ophelia is what she seems, this dirty-minded world of murder, incest, lust, adultery, is no place for her. Were she "as chaste as ice, as pure as snow," she could not escape its calumny. And if she is not what she seems, then a nunnery in its other sense of brothel is relevant to her. In the scene that follows he treats her as if she were indeed an inmate of a brothel.

Likewise, from Hamlet's point of view, there is the enigma of the king. If the ghost is *only* an appearance, then possibly the king's appearance is reality. He must try it further. By means of a second and different kind of "apparition," the play within the play, he does so. But then, immediately after, he stumbles on the king at prayer. This appearance has a relish of salvation in it. If the king dies now, his soul may yet be saved. Yet actually, as we know, the king's efforts to come to terms with heaven have been unavailing; his words fly up, his thoughts remain below. If Hamlet means the conventional revenger's reasons that he gives for sparing Claudius, it was the perfect moment not to spare him—when the sinner was acknowledging his guilt, yet unrepentant. The perfect moment, but it was hidden, like so much else in the play, behind an arras.

There are two arrases in his mother's room. Hamlet thrusts his sword through one of them. Now at last he has got to the heart of the evil, or so he thinks. But now it is the wrong man; now he himself is a murderer. The other arras he stabs through with his words—like daggers, says the queen. He makes her shrink under the contrast he points between her present husband and his father. But as the play now stands (matters are somewhat clearer in the bad Quarto), it is hard to be sure how far the queen grasps the fact that her second husband is the murderer of her first. And it is hard to say what may be signified by her inability to see the ghost, who now for the last time appears. In one sense at least, the ghost is the supreme reality, representative of the hidden ultimate power, in Bradley's terms—witnessing from beyond the grave against this hollow world. Yet the man who is capable of seeing through to this reality, the queen thinks is mad. "To whom do you speak this?" she cries to her son. "Do you see nothing there?" he asks, incredulous. And she replies: "Nothing at all; yet all that is I see." Here certainly we have the imperturbable self-confidence of the worldly world, its layers on layers of habituation, so that when the reality is before its very eyes it cannot detect its presence.

Like mystery, this problem of reality is central to the play and written deep into its idiom. Shakespeare's favorite terms in *Hamlet* are words of ordinary usage that pose the question of appearances in a fundamental form. "Apparition" I have already mentioned. Another term is "seems." When we say, as Ophelia says of Hamlet leaving her closet, "He seem'd to find his way without his eyes," we mean one thing. When we say, as Hamlet says to his mother in the first court-scene, "Seems, Madam! . . . I know not 'seems,'" we mean another. And when we say, as Hamlet says to Horatio before the play within the play, "And after, we will both our judgments join In censure of his seeming," we mean both at once. The ambiguities of "seem" coil and uncoil throughout this play, and over

against them is set the idea of "seeing." So Hamlet challenges the
king in his triumphant letter announcing his return to Denmark:
"Tomorrow shall I beg leave to see your kingly eyes." Yet "seeing"
itself can be ambiguous, as we recognize from Hamlet's uncertainty
about the ghost; or from that statement of his mother's already
quoted: "Nothing at all; yet all that is I see."

Another term of like importance is "assume." What we assume
may be what we are not: "The de'il hath power T' assume a pleasing shape." But it may be what we are: "If it assume my noble
father's person, I'll speak to it." And it may be what we are not
yet, but would become; thus Hamlet advises his mother, "Assume
a virtue, if you have it not." The perplexity in the word points to
a real perplexity in Hamlet's and our own experience. We assume
our habits—and habits are like costumes, as the word implies: "My
father in his habit as he liv'd!" Yet these habits become ourselves
in time: "That monster, custom, who all sense doth eat Of habits
evil, is angel yet in this, That to the use of actions fair and good
He likewise gives a frock or livery That aptly is put on."

Two other terms I wish to instance are "put on" and "shape."
The shape of something is the form under which we are accustomed
to apprehend it: "Do you see yonder cloud that's almost in shape
of a camel?" But a shape may also be a disguise—even, in Shakespeare's
time, an actor's costume or an actor's role. This is the meaning
when the king says to Laertes as they lay the plot against Hamlet's
life: "Weigh what convenience both of time and means May fit us to
our shape." "Put on" supplies an analogous ambiguity. Shakespeare's
mind seems to worry this phrase in the play much as Hamlet's
mind worries the problem of acting in a world of surfaces, or the
king's mind worries the meaning of Hamlet's transformation. Hamlet
has put an antic disposition on, that the king knows. But what does
"put on" mean? A mask, or a frock or livery—our "habit"? The
king is left guessing, and so are we.

What is found in the play's key terms is also found in its imagery.
Miss Spurgeon has called attention to a pattern of disease images
in *Hamlet,* to which I shall return. But the play has other patterns
equally striking. One of these, as my earlier quotations hint, is
based on clothes. In the world of surfaces to which Shakespeare exposes us in Hamlet, clothes are naturally a factor of importance.
"The apparel oft proclaims the man," Polonius assures Laertes,
cataloguing maxims in the young man's ear as he is about to leave
for Paris. Oft, but not always. And so he sends his man Reynaldo
to look into Laertes' life there—even, if need be, to put a false
dress of accusation upon his son ("What forgeries you please"), the
better by indirections to find directions out. On the same grounds,

he takes Hamlet's vows to Ophelia as false apparel. They are bawds, he tells her—or if we do not like Theobald's emendation, they are bonds—in masquerade, "Not of that dye which their investments show, But mere implorators of unholy suits."

This breach between the outer and the inner stirs no special emotion in Polonius, because he is always either behind an arras or prying into one, but it shakes Hamlet to the core. Here so recently was his mother in her widow's weeds, the tears still flushing in her gallèd eyes; yet now within a month, a little month, before even her funeral shoes are old, she has married with his uncle. Her mourning was all clothes. Not so his own, he bitterly replies, when she asks him to cast his "nighted color off." "Tis not alone my inky cloak, good mother"—and not alone, he adds, the sighs, the tears, the dejected havior of the visage—"that can denote me truly."

> These indeed seem,
> For they are actions that a man might play;
> But I have that within which passes show;
> These but the trappings and the suits of woe.

What we must not overlook here is Hamlet's visible attire, giving the verbal imagery a theatrical extension. Hamlet's apparel now is his inky cloak, mark of his grief for his father, mark also of his character as a man of melancholy, mark possibly too of his being one in whom appearance and reality are attuned. Later, in his madness, with his mind disordered, he will wear his costume in a corresponding disarray, the disarray that Ophelia describes so vividly to Polonius and that producers of the play rarely give sufficient heed to: "Lord Hamlet with his doublet all unbrac'd, No hat upon his head; his stockings foul'd, Ungarter'd, and down-gyved to his ankle." Here the only question will be, as with the madness itself, how much is studied, how much is real. Still later, by a third costume, the simple traveler's garb in which we find him new come from shipboard, Shakespeare will show us that we have a third aspect of the man.

A second pattern of imagery springs from terms of painting: the paints, the colorings, the varnishes that may either conceal or, as in the painter's art, reveal. Art in Claudius conceals. "The harlot's cheek," he tells us in his one aside, "beautied with plastering art, Is not more ugly to the thing that helps it Than is my deed to my most painted word." Art in Ophelia, loosed to Hamlet in the episode already noticed to which this speech of the king's is prelude, is more complex. She looks so beautiful—"the celestial, and my soul's idol, the most beautified Ophelia," Hamlet has called her in his love letter. But now, what does beautified mean? Perfected with all the innocent beauties of a lovely woman? Or "beautied" like the harlot's cheek? "I have heard of your paintings too, well enough. God hath given you one face, and you make yourselves another."

Yet art, differently used, may serve the truth. By using an "image" (his own word) of a murder done in Vienna, Hamlet cuts through to the king's guilt; holds "as 'twere, the mirror up to nature," shows "virtue her own feature, scorn her own image, and the very age and body of the time"—which is out of joint—"his form and pressure." Something similar he does again in his mother's bedroom, painting for her in words "the rank sweat of an enseamed bed," making her recoil in horror from his "counterfeit presentment of two brothers," and holding, if we may trust a stage tradition, his father's picture beside his uncle's. Here again the verbal imagery is realized visually on the stage.

The most pervasive of Shakespeare's image patterns in this play, however, is the pattern evolved around the three words, show, act, play. "Show" seems to be Shakespeare's unifying image in *Hamlet*. Through it he pulls together and exhibits in a single focus much of the diverse material in his play. The ideas of seeming, assuming, and putting on; the images of clothing, painting, mirroring; the episode of the dumb show and the play within the play; the characters of Polonius, Laertes, Ophelia, Claudius, Gertrude, Rosencrantz and Guildenstern, Hamlet himself—all these at one time or another, and usually more than once, are drawn into the range of implications flung round the play by "show."

"Act," on the other hand, I take to be the play's radical metaphor. It distills the various perplexities about the character of reality into a residual perplexity about the character of an act. What, this play asks again and again, is an act? What is its relation to the inner act, the intent? "If I drown myself wittingly," says the clown in the graveyard, "it argues an act, and an act hath three branches; it is to act, to do, to perform." Or again, the play asks, how does action relate to passion, that "laps'd in time and passion" I can let "go by Th' important acting of your dread command"; and to thought, which can so sickly o'er the native hue of resolution that "enterprises of great pitch and moment With this regard their currents turn awry, And lose the name of action"; and to words, which are not acts, and so we dare not be content to unpack our hearts with them, and yet are acts of a sort, for we may speak daggers though we use none. Or still again, how does an act (a deed) relate to an act (a pretense)? For an action may be nothing but pretense. So Polonius readying Ophelia for the interview with Hamlet, with "pious action," as he phrases it, "sugar[s] o'er The devil himself." Or it may not be a pretense, yet not what it appears. So Hamlet spares the king, finding him in an act that has some "relish of salvation in 't." Or it may be a pretense that is also the first foothold of a new reality, as when we assume a virtue though we have it not. Or it may be a pretense that is actually a mirroring of reality, like the play within the play, or the tragedy of *Hamlet*.

To this network of implications, the third term, play, adds an additional dimension. "Play" is a more precise word, in Elizabethan parlance at least, for all the elements in *Hamlet* that pertain to the art of the theatre; and it extends their field of reference till we see that every major personage in the tragedy is a player in some sense, and every major episode a play. The court plays, Hamlet plays, the players play, Rosencrantz and Guildenstern try to play on Hamlet, though they cannot play on his recorders—here we have an extension to a musical sense. And the final duel, by a further extension, becomes itself a play, in which everyone but Claudius and Laertes plays his role in ignorance: "The queen desires you to show some gentle entertainment to Laertes before you fall to play." "I . . . will this brother's wager frankly play." "Give him the cup."—"I'll play this bout first."

The full extension of this theme is best evidenced in the play within the play itself. Here, in the bodily presence of these traveling players, bringing with them the latest playhouse gossip out of London, we have suddenly a situation that tends to dissolve the normal barriers between the fictive and the real. For here on the stage before us is a play of false appearances in which an actor called the player-king is playing. But there is also on the stage, Claudius, another player-king, who is a spectator of this player. And there is on the stage, besides, a prince who is a spectator of both these player-kings and who plays with great intensity a player's role himself. And around these kings and that prince is a group of courtly spectators—Gertrude, Rosencrantz, Guildenstern, Polonius, and the rest—and they, as we have come to know, are players too. And lastly there are ourselves, an audience watching all these audiences who are also players. Where, it may suddenly occur to us to ask, does the playing end? Which *are* the guilty creatures sitting at a play? When is an act not an "act"?

The mysteriousness of Hamlet's world, while it pervades the trage- dy, finds its point of greatest dramatic concentration in the first act, and its symbol in the first scene. The problems of appearance and reality also pervade the play as a whole, but come to a climax in Acts II and III, and possibly their best symbol is the play within the play. Our third attribute, though again it is one that crops out everywhere, reaches its full development in Acts IV and V. It is not easy to find an appropriate name for this attribute, but perhaps "mortality" will serve, if we remember to mean by mortality the heartache and the thousand natural shocks that flesh is heir to, not simply death.

The powerful sense of mortality in *Hamlet* is conveyed to us, I think, in three ways. First, there is the play's emphasis on human weakness, the instability of human purpose, the subjection of humanity to fortune—all that we might call the aspect of failure in man. Hamlet opens this theme in Act I, when he describes how from that single blemish, perhaps not even the victim's fault, a man's whole character may take corruption. Claudius dwells on it again, to an extent that goes far beyond the needs of the occasion, while engaged in seducing Laertes to step behind the arras of a seemer's world and dispose of Hamlet by a trick. Time qualifies everything, Claudius says, including love, including purpose. As for love—it has a "plurisy" in it and dies of its own too much. As for purpose—"That we would do, We should do when we would, for this 'would' changes, And hath abatements and delays as many As there are tongues, are hands, are accidents; And then this 'should' is like a spendthrift's sigh, That hurts by easing." The player-king, in his long speeches to his queen in the play within the play, sets the matter in a still darker light. She means these protestations of undying love, he knows, but our purposes depend on our memory, and our memory fades fast. Or else, he suggests, we propose something to ourselves in a condition of strong feeling, but then the feeling goes, and with it the resolve. Or else our fortunes change, he adds, and with these our loves: "The great man down, you mark his favorite flies." The subjection of human aims to fortune is a reiterated theme in *Hamlet,* as subsequently in *Lear.* Fortune is the harlot goddess in whose secret parts men like Rosencrantz and Guildenstern live and thrive; the strumpet who threw down Troy and Hecuba and Priam; the outrageous foe whose slings and arrows a man of principle must suffer or seek release in suicide. Horatio suffers them with composure: he is one of the blessed few "Whose blood and judgment are so well co-mingled That they are not a pipe for fortune's finger To sound what stop she please." For Hamlet the task is of a greater difficulty.

Next, and intimately related to this matter of infirmity, is the emphasis on infection—the ulcer, the hidden abscess, "th' imposthume of much wealth and peace That inward breaks and shows no cause without Why the man dies." Miss Spurgeon, who was the first to call attention to this aspect of the play, has well remarked that so far as Shakespeare's pictorial imagination is concerned, the problem in *Hamlet* is not a problem of the will and reason, "of a mind too philosophical or a nature temperamentally unfitted to act quickly," nor even a problem of an individual at all. Rather, it is a condition—"a condition for which the individual himself is apparently not responsible, any more than the sick man is to blame for the infection which strikes and devours him, but which, nevertheless, in its course and development, impartially and relentlessly, annihilates him and others, innocent and guilty alike." "That," she adds, "is the tragedy of *Hamlet,* as it is perhaps the chief tragic mystery of life." This is a perceptive comment, for it reminds us that Hamlet's situation is mainly not of his own manufacture, as are the situations of Shakespeare's other tragic heroes. He has inherited it; he is "born to set it right."

We must not, however, neglect to add to this what another student of Shakespeare's imagery has noticed—that the infection in Denmark is presented alternatively as poison. Here, of course, responsibility is implied, for the poisoner of the play is Claudius. The juice he pours into the ear of the elder Hamlet is a combined poison and disease, a "leperous distilment" that curds "the thin and whole-some blood." From this fatal center, unwholesomeness spreads out till there is something rotten in all Denmark. Hamlet tells us that his "wit's diseased," the queen speaks of her "sick soul," the king is troubled by "the hectic" in his blood, Laertes meditates revenge to warm "the sickness in my heart," the people of the kingdom grow "muddied, Thick and unwholesome in their thoughts"; and even Ophelia's madness is said to be "the poison of deep grief." In the end, all save Ophelia die of that poison in a literal as well as figurative sense.

But the chief form in which the theme of mortality reaches us, it seems to me, is as a profound consciousness of loss. Hamlet's father expresses something of the kind when he tells Hamlet how his "most seeming-virtuous queen," betraying a love which "was of that dignity That it went hand in hand even with the vow I made to her in marriage," had chosen to "decline Upon a wretch whose natural gifts were poor To those of mine." "O Hamlet, what a falling off was there!" Ophelia expresses it again, on hearing Hamlet's denuncia-tion of love and woman in the nunnery scene, which she takes to be the product of a disordered brain:

> O what a noble mind is here o'erthrown!
> The courtier's, soldier's, scholar's, eye, tongue, sword;
> Th' expectancy and rose of the fair state,
> The glass of fashion and the mould of form,
> Th' observ'd of all observers, quite, quite down!

The passage invites us to remember that we have never actually seen such a Hamlet—that his mother's marriage has brought a falling off in him before we meet him. And then there is that further falling off, if I may call it so, when Ophelia too goes mad—"Divided from herself and her fair judgment, Without the which we are pictures, or mere beasts."

Time was, the play keeps reminding us, when Denmark was a different place. That was before Hamlet's mother took off "the rose From the fair forehead of an innocent love" and set a blister there. Hamlet then was still "th' expectancy and rose of the fair state"; Ophelia, the "rose of May." For Denmark was a garden then, when his father ruled. There had been something heroic about his father—a king who met the threats to Denmark in open battle, fought with Norway, smote the sledded Polacks on the ice, slew the elder Fortinbras in an honorable trial of strength. There had been something godlike about his father too: "Hyperion's curls, the front of Jove himself, An eye like Mars . . . , A station like the herald Mercury." But, the ghost reveals, a serpent was in the garden, and "the serpent that did sting thy father's life Now wears his crown." The martial virtues are put by now. The threats to Denmark are attended to by policy, by agents working deviously for and through an uncle. The moral virtues are put by too. Hyperion's throne is occupied by "a vice of kings," "a king of shreds and patches"; Hyperion's bed, by a satyr, a paddock, a bat, a gib, a bloat king with reechy kisses. The garden is unweeded now, and "grows to seed; things rank and gross in nature Possess it merely." Even in himself he feels the taint, the taint of being his mother's son; and that other taint, from an earlier garden, of which he admonishes Ophelia: "Our virtue cannot so inoculate our old stock but we shall relish of it." "Why wouldst thou be a breeder of sinners?" "What should such fellows as I do crawling between earth and heaven?"

"Hamlet is painfully aware," says Professor Tillyard, "of the baffling human predicament between the angels and the beasts, between the glory of having been made in God's image and the incrimination of being descended from fallen Adam." To this we may add, I think, that Hamlet is more than aware of it; he exemplifies it; and it is for this reason that his problem appeals to us so powerfully as an image of our own.

Hamlet's problem, in its crudest form, is simply the problem of the avenger; he must carry out the injunction of the ghost and kill the king. But this problem, as I ventured to suggest at the outset, is presented in terms of a certain kind of world. The ghost's injunction to act becomes so inextricably bound up for Hamlet with the character of the world in which the action must be taken—its mysteriousness, its baffling appearances, its deep consciousness of infection, frailty, and loss—that he cannot come to terms with either without coming to terms with both.

When we first see him in the play, he is clearly a very young man, sensitive and idealistic, suffering the first shock of growing up. He

has taken the garden at face value, we might say, supposing mankind to be only a little lower than the angels. Now in his mother's
hasty and incestuous marriage, he discovers evidence of something
else, something bestial—though even a beast, he thinks, would have
mourned longer. Then comes the revelation of the ghost, bringing
a second shock. Not so much because he now knows that his serpent-
uncle killed his father; his prophetic soul had almost suspected this.
Not entirely, even, because he knows now how far below the angels
humanity has fallen in his mother, and how lust—these were the
ghost's words—"though to a radiant angel link'd Will sate itself in a
celestial bed, And prey on garbage." Rather, because he now sees
everywhere, but especially in his own nature, the general taint, taking
from life its meaning, from woman her integrity, from the will its
strength, turning reason into madness. "Why wouldst thou be a
breeder of sinners?" "What should such fellows as I do crawling between earth and heaven?" Hamlet is not the first young man to have
felt the heavy and the weary weight of all this unintelligible world;
and, like the others, he must come to terms with it.

The ghost's injunction to revenge unfolds a different facet of his
problem. The young man growing up is not to be allowed simply
to endure a rotten world, he must also act in it. Yet how to begin,
among so many enigmatic surfaces? Even Claudius, whom he now
knows to be the core of the ulcer, has a plausible exterior. And
around Claudius, swathing the evil out of sight, he encounters all
those other exteriors, as we have seen. Some of them already deeply
infected beneath, like his mother. Some noble, but marked for infection, like Laertes. Some not particularly corrupt but infinitely
corruptible, like Rosencrantz and Guildenstern; some mostly weak
and foolish like Polonius and Osric. Some, like Ophelia, innocent,
yet in their innocence still serving to "skin and film the ulcerous
place."

And this is not all. The act required of him, though retributive
justice, is one that necessarily involves the doer in the general guilt.
Not only because it involves a killing; but because to get at the
world of seeming one sometimes has to use its weapons. He himself,
before he finishes, has become a player, has put an antic disposition
on, has killed a man—the wrong man—has helped drive Ophelia
mad, and has sent two friends of his youth to death, mining below
their mines, and hoisting the engineer with his own petard. He
had never meant to dirty himself with these things, but from the
moment of the ghost's challenge to act, this dirtying was inevitable.
It is the condition of living at all in such a world. To quote Polonius,
who knew that world so well, men become "a little soil'd i' th'
working." Here is another matter with which Hamlet has to come
to terms.

Human infirmity—all that I have discussed with reference to instability, infection, loss—supplies the problem with its third phase.
Hamlet has not only to accept the mystery of man's condition between the angels and the brutes, and not only to act in a perplexing
and soiling world. He has also to act within the human limits—
"with shabby equipment always deteriorating," if I may adapt some
phrases from Eliot's "East Coker," "In the general mess of im-
precision of feeling, Undisciplined squads of emotion." Hamlet is
aware of that fine poise of body and mind, feeling and thought,
that suits the action to the word, the word to the action; that acquires
and begets a temperance in the very torrent, tempest, and whirlwind
of passion; but he cannot at first achieve it in himself. He vacillates
between undisciplined squads of emotion and thinking too precisely
on the event. He learns to his cost how easily action can be lost in
"acting," and loses it there for a time himself. But these again are
only the terms of every man's life. As Anatole France reminds us
in a now famous apostrophe to Hamlet: "What one of us thinks
without contradiction and acts without incoherence? What one of
us is not mad? What one of us does not say with a mixture of pity,
comradeship, admiration, and horror, Goodnight, sweet Prince!"

In the last act of the play (or so it seems to me, for I know there
can be differences on this point), Hamlet accepts his world and we
discover a different man. Shakespeare does not outline for us the
process of acceptance any more than he had done with Romeo or
was to do with Othello. But he leads us strongly to expect an altered
Hamlet, and then, in my opinion, provides him. We must recall
that at this point Hamlet has been absent from the stage during
several scenes, and that such absences in Shakespearean tragedy usually
warn us to be on the watch for a new phase in the development of the
character. It is so when we leave King Lear in Gloucester's farm-
house and find him again in Dover fields. It is so when we leave
Macbeth at the witches' cave and rejoin him at Dunsinane, hearing
of the armies that beset it. Furthermore, and this is an important
matter in the theatre—especially important in a play in which the
symbolism of clothing has figured largely—Hamlet now looks different. He is wearing a different dress—probably, as Granville-Barker
thinks, his "sea-gown scarf'd" about him, but in any case no longer
the disordered costume of his antic disposition. The effect is not
entirely dissimilar to that in *Lear,* when the old king wakes out
of his madness to find fresh garments on him.

Still more important, Hamlet displays a considerable change of
mood. This is not a matter of the way we take the passage about
defying augury, as Mr. Tillyard among others seems to think. It
is a matter of Hamlet's whole deportment, in which I feel we may
legitimately see the deportment of a man who has been "illuminated"

in the tragic sense. Bradley's term for it is fatalism, but if this is what we wish to call it, we must at least acknowledge that it is fatalism of a very distinctive kind—a kind that Shakespeare has been willing to touch with the associations of the saying in St. Matthew about the fall of a sparrow, and with Hamlet's recognition that a divinity shapes our ends. The point is not that Hamlet has suddenly become religious; he has been religious all through the play. The point is that he has now learned, and accepted, the boundaries in which human action, human judgment, are enclosed.

Till his return from the voyage he had been trying to act beyond these, had been encroaching on the role of providence, if I may exaggerate to make a vital point. He had been too quick to take the burden of the whole world and its condition upon his limited and finite self. Faced with a task of sufficient difficulty in its own right, he had dilated it into a cosmic problem—as indeed every task is, but if we think about this too precisely we cannot act at all. The whole time is out of joint, he feels, and in his young man's egocentricity, he will set it right. Hence he misjudges Ophelia, seeing in her only a breeder of sinners. Hence he misjudges himself, seeing himself a vermin crawling between earth and heaven. Hence he takes it upon himself to be his mother's conscience, though the ghost has warned that this is no fit task for him, and returns to repeat the warning: "Leave her to heaven, And to those thorns that in her bosom lodge." Even with the king, Hamlet has sought to play at God. *He* it must be who decides the issue of Claudius's salvation, saving him for a more damnable occasion. Now, he has learned that there are limits to the before and after that human reason can comprehend. Rashness, even, is sometimes good. Through rashness he has saved his life from the commission for his death, "and prais'd be rashness for it." This happy circumstance and the unexpected arrival of the pirate ship make it plain that the roles of life are not entirely self-assigned. "There is a divinity that shapes our ends, Rough-hew them how we will." Hamlet is ready now for what may happen, seeking neither to foreknow it nor avoid it. "If it be now, 'tis not to come; if it be not to come, it will be now; if it be not now, yet it will come: the readiness is all."

The crucial evidence of Hamlet's new frame of mind, as I understand it, is the graveyard scene. Here, in its ultimate symbol, he confronts, recognizes, and accepts the condition of being man. It is not simply that he now accepts death, though Shakespeare shows him accepting it in ever more poignant forms: first, in the imagined persons of the politician, the courtier, and the lawyer, who laid their little schemes "to circumvent God," as Hamlet puts it, but now lie here; then in Yorick, whom he knew and played with as a child; and then in Ophelia. This last death tears from him a final cry of passion, but the striking contrast between his behavior and Laertes's reveals how deeply he has changed.

Still, it is not the fact of death that invests this scene with its peculiar power. It is instead the haunting mystery of life itself that Hamlet's speeches point to, holding in its inscrutable folds those other mysteries that he has wrestled with so long. These he now knows for what they are, and lays them by. The mystery of evil is present here—for this is after all the universal graveyard, where, as the clown says humorously, he holds up Adam's profession; where the scheming politician, the hollow courtier, the tricky lawyer, the emperor and the clown and the beautiful young maiden, all come together in an emblem of the world; where even, Hamlet murmurs, one might expect to stumble on "Cain's jawbone, that did the first murther." The mystery of reality is here too—for death puts the question, "What is real?" in its irreducible form, and in the end uncovers all appearances: "Is this the fine of his fines and the recovery of his recoveries, to have his fine pate full of fine dirt?" "Now get you to my lady's chamber, and tell her, let her paint an inch thick, to this favor she must come." Or if we need more evidence of this mystery, there is the anger of Laertes at the lack of ceremonial trappings, and the ambiguous character of Ophelia's own death. "Is she to be buried in Christian burial when she wilfully seeks her own salvation?" asks the gravedigger. And last of all, but most pervasive of all, there is the mystery of human limitation. The grotesque nature of man's little joys, his big ambitions. The fact that the man who used to bear us on his back is now a skull that smells; that the noble dust of Alexander somewhere plugs a bung-hole; that "Imperious Caesar, dead and turn'd to clay, Might stop a hole to keep the wind away." Above all, the fact that a pit of clay is "meet" for such a guest as man, as the gravedigger tells us in his song, and yet that, despite all frailties, and limitations, "That skull had a tongue in it and could sing once."

After the graveyard and what it indicates has come to pass in him, we know that Hamlet is ready for the final contest of mighty opposites. He accepts the world as it is, the world as a duel, in which, whether we know it or not, evil holds the poisoned rapier and the poisoned chalice waits; and in which, if we win at all, it costs not less than everything. I think we understand by the close of Shakespeare's *Hamlet* why it is that unlike the other tragic heroes he is given a soldier's rites upon the stage. For as William Butler Yeats once said, "Why should we honor those who die on the field of battle? A man may show as reckless a courage in entering into the abyss of himself."

An Approach to *Hamlet*

by *L. C. Knights*

Hamlet is a man who in the face of life and of death can make no affirmation, and it may well be that this irresolution—which goes far deeper than irresolution about the performance of a specific act—this fundamental doubt, explains the great appeal of the play in modern times. The point has been made by D. G. James in *The Dream of Learning*. Shakespeare's play, he says, "is an image of modernity, of the soul without clear belief losing its way, and bringing itself and others to great distress and finally to disaster"; it is "a tragedy not of excessive thought but of defeated thought," and Hamlet himself is "a man caught in ethical and metaphysical uncertainties." Now I am sure that Mr. James is right in emphasizing the element of scepticism in Hamlet's makeup—the weighing of alternative possibilities in such a way as to make choice between them virtually impossible; and I sympathize with his wish "to elevate Hamlet's intellectual distresses to an equality in importance with his emotional state," for "the strength of the emotional shock he has suffered is equalled by the weakness of his mind in the face of difficult moral and metaphysical issues. Hamlet was, after all, an intellectual." But at the same time I feel that the play incites us to a closer examination of the intimate and complex relationship of thought and feeling, of intellectual bafflement and certain aspects of the emotional life; in the play before us the dominant emotions are activated by certain specific shocks but they cannot be attributed solely to these.

In an essay called *Hamlet and Don Quixote* Ivan Turgenev took up this very question of Hamlet's scepticism, but instead of regarding it as a purely intellectual matter he related it to central attitudes of the self, to a certain moral inadequacy.

Hamlet (he says) is, beyond all things else, analysis and egoism, scepticism personified.

From An Approach to Hamlet, *by L. C. Knights (Stanford: Stanford University Press, 1961; London: Chatto & Windus, Ltd., 1960), pp. 55-69. Copyright © 1960 by L. C. Knights. Reprinted by permission of the author and the publishers. This selection is from Chapter III.*

He lives only to himself. He is an egoist, and as such can have no faith
in himself; for no man can have faith save in that which is outside self
and above self.

None the less Hamlet clings tenaciously to this "I," this self in which
he has no faith. It is a centre to which he constantly returns because he
finds that in this world there is nothing to which he can cleave with all
his soul.

A sceptic, Hamlet is preoccupied with his own personality; but he
ponders its strategical situation, not its duties.[1]

In other words, Hamlet is one of those in whom "the 'I' in the individual" preponderates, not "something outside the 'I,' which the
individual prefers to the 'I.'" Now I think that this also is true, but
again, taken in isolation, it does not quite do justice to the imaginative
facts as we know them; for what it ignores is the pain and the passion—the genuine pain of loss and the genuine passion of revulsion
against what is really evil. Max Plowman perhaps, in an essay called
"Some Values in *Hamlet*" (reprinted in *The Right to Live*) brings
us nearer the mark when he speaks of Hamlet as one who has risen
above the level of the merely instinctive—the level at which most
of those who surround him live, and at which revenge is an obvious
duty—but who has not risen to full and adequate consciousness.

For as we come to objective consciousness, we realize that no one lives
to himself: we know, in fact, that life consists in the interplay of subject
and object, and that the completely isolated person can only be said to
exist; for to be completely isolated is to lack intercourse with anything
outside the self.

Hamlet, on the other hand, is in the intermediate state of self-
consciousness, "the most unlovable of all conditions": "Hamlet is
self-conscious man in an unconscious world"; what he suffers from
is "a fixation of self-consciousness." The point, you see, is very close
to that made by Turgenev. But there is this difference: Max Plowman sees Hamlet's state as one phase in a development that is not
peculiar to any one individual; however far Hamlet goes astray he
starts from a point through which everyone—or almost everyone—
must pass who is to rise above the instinctive and unself-knowing
to that state of genuine being for which one name is consciousness.

I think we shall not be far wrong if, in seeking to account for

[1] I quote from the translation by Robert Nichols (London: Henderson, 1930). I
was reminded of the existence of Turgenev's little known essay by the reference in
Miss Rebecca West's *The Court and the Castle: the Interaction of Political and Religious Ideas in Imaginative Literature:* in the chapters on *Hamlet* Miss West has
some interesting things to say about current misconceptions of the play.

Hamlet's paralysis, his inability to affirm, we give special prominence
to his isolation and self-consciousness. Now consciousness, as distinguished from Hamlet's self-consciousness, is dependent upon love
and relationship, and the name that Blake gave to consciousness, as
Max Plowman remarks in this same essay, is the Imagination. Hamlet,
for all his ranging mind and his nervous susceptibility, is not in this
sense imaginative; in Blakean terms he is in the power of his Spectre.

> Each Man is in his Spectre's power
> Untill the arrival of that hour,
> When his Humanity awake
> And cast his own Spectre into the Lake.

These lines occur in the Rossetti MS. Looking up other instances of
"Spectre" in the Index to the edition of the Prophetic Writings by
Sloss and Wallis, I found (what I had not noticed before) that Blake
also used them in *Jerusalem:* in the drawing showing Albion in
despair (Plate 41) they are engraved in reverse on the stone at the
feet of the seated bowed figure, his face covered by his hands; and
it is not irrelevant to our present concerns to notice that the passage
immediately following this illustration begins,

> Thus Albion sat, studious of others in his pale disease,
> Brooding on evil . . .

I hope you will not misunderstand me. I do not think that Shakespeare
wrote *Hamlet* as an esoteric commentary on Blake's Prophetic Books,
or that Hamlet's Ghost is to be identified with Blake's Spectre. It
is simply that both poets had some comparable insights, and the
one may be used to bring out the meaning of the other. Blake's
Spectre is the rationalizing faculty, self-centered and moralistic, working in isolation from the other powers and potentialities of the mind.
Unless redeemed by Los, the Imagination, in dealing with the self
and with others it can only criticize and accuse, creating around itself
what Wordsworth was to call "a universe of death."

Hamlet, "studious of others in his pale disease, Brooding on evil,"
is, in this sense, in the power of his Spectre. He is indeed, as Mr.
James and many others have insisted, an intellectual, a man given to
reason and reflection. But what Shakespeare is bringing in question
in this play is what it means to be an intellectual in any but a sterile
sense, the conditions on which this capability can be indeed "god-
like." Hamlet's intellectuality, the working of his mind, is largely
at the service of attitudes of rejection and disgust that are indis-
criminate in their working. Let me repeat what I have said before:
the Denmark of this play is indeed an unweeded garden; there are
facts enough to justify almost everything Hamlet says about this

world; but what we have to take note of is not only what he says but a particular vibration in the saying. We can define this in relation to his self-disgust, his spreading sexual nausea, and his condemnation of others.

When Hamlet first reveals himself in soliloquy it is in terms of a revulsion for which the preceding court scene has in some measure prepared us.

> O! that this too too sullied flesh would melt,
> Thaw and resolve itself into a dew . . .

His flesh is sullied because it is the flesh of a woman who, in a matter of weeks from the death of her first husband, has married her husband's brother: "a beast, that wants discourse of reason, Would have mourn'd longer"; she is moreover infatuated with a man who clearly has some of the qualities of the "satyr" that Hamlet attributes to him. These are données of the case, and it need occasion no surprise when Hamlet declares that "virtue cannot so inoculate our old stock but we shall relish of it." This sense of being tainted is both explicable and natural, but Shakespeare is careful to show us that there is more than this involved in Hamlet's bitter judgment on himself. The disgust with the self that we must all at some time feel, for whatever cause, changes its quality when it is used to shock and damage, as Hamlet uses it to damage his dawning relationship with Ophelia.

Hamlet. . . . if you be honest and fair, your honesty should admit no discourse to your beauty.

Ophelia. Could beauty, my lord, have better commerce than with honesty?

Hamlet. Ay, truly; for the power of beauty will sooner transform honesty from what it is to a bawd than the force of honesty can translate beauty into his likeness; this was sometime a paradox, but now the time gives it proof. I did love you once.

Ophelia. Indeed, my lord, you made me believe so.

Hamlet. You should not have believed me; for virtue cannot so inoculate our old stock but we shall relish of it; I loved you not.

Ophelia. I was the more deceived.

Hamlet. Get thee to a nunnery; why wouldst thou be a breeder of sinners? I am myself indifferent honest; but yet I could accuse me of such things that it were better my mother had not borne me. I am very proud, revengeful, ambitious; with more offences at my beck than I have thoughts to put them in, imagination to give them shape, or time to act them in. What should such fellows as I do crawling between heaven and earth? We are arrant knaves all; believe none of us. Go thy ways to a nunnery.

We may for the moment leave on one side the question of what
Hamlet, in this and similar passages, is doing to another's consciousness—driving a wedge into it so that it too must inevitably suffer
—though that Shakespeare was not indifferent to it we know from
Ophelia's madness and her—apparently half-sought—death. But if we
ask whether what Hamlet says or implies about himself is mature
self-knowledge or, as Turgenev suggests, mere self-flagellation, I do
not think that the answer can be in any doubt. "I am very proud,
revengeful, ambitious; with more offences at my beck than I have
thoughts to put them in, imagination to give them shape, or time
to act them in." This, it has been said, "sounds very terrible, but
considered carefully it amounts to nothing." What it means, it
seems to me, is that Hamlet is in a state of panic recoil not only
from sex but from those aggressions and self-assertive drives that
sooner or later we have to come to terms with and put to constructive
use. Many of Shakespeare's characters, it is true, are constrained to
take stock of things within of which they are bitterly ashamed.
There is, for example, Lear:

> Poor naked wretches, whereso'er you are,
> That bide the pelting of this pitiless storm,
> How shall your houseless heads and unfed sides,
> Your loop'd and window'd raggedness, defend you
> From seasons such as this? O! I have ta'en
> Too little care of this. Take physic, pomp . . .

Or there is Posthumus, in prison and awaiting death:

> My conscience, thou art fetter'd
> More than my shanks and wrists; you good gods, give me
> The penitent instrument to pick that bolt;
> Then, free for ever! Is't enough I am sorry?
> So children temporal fathers do appease;
> Gods are more full of mercy. Must I repent?
> I cannot do it better than in gyves,
> Desir'd more than constrained; to satisfy,
> If of my freedom 'tis the main part, take
> No stricter render of me than my all . . .
>   . . . and so, great powers,
> If you will take this audit, take this life,
> And cancel these cold bonds. O Imogen!
> I'll speak to thee in silence.

To say that there is an absolute difference of tone and intention between these self-communings and anything that Hamlet may say

by way of self-condemnation is to comment on the obvious. When indeed he has anything real to repent of, his self-exculpatory manner suggests something like obliviousness to what he has done. Of the murder of Polonius:

> For this same lord,
> I do repent; but heaven hath pleased it so,
> To punish me with this, and this with me,
> That I must be their scourge and minister . . .

—to be followed shortly by "I'll lug the guts into the neighbour room." Of his unseemly ranting in Ophelia's grave with Laertes, whose father he has killed, and for whose sister's death he is at least in part to blame:

> What I have done,
> That might your nature, honour, and exception
> Roughly awake, I here proclaim was madness.
> Was't Hamlet wrong'd Laertes? Never Hamlet;
> If Hamlet from himself be ta'en away,
> And when he's not himself does wrong Laertes,
> Then Hamlet does it not; Hamlet denies it.
> Who does it then? His madness; if't be so,
> Hamlet is of the faction that is wrong'd;
> His madness is poor Hamlet's enemy.

One can hardly resist the feeling that some of the energy that Hamlet expends in unpacking his heart with words might more profitably have been directed—and with more humility—towards a stricter accounting of his share in the harm done to others.

It is much the same with his sexual insistence. Grant that he is deeply wounded—as who would not be?—by his mother's conduct:

> why, she would hang on him [her first husband]
> As if increase of appetite had grown
> By what it fed on . . .
>
> O, most wicked speed, to post
> With such dexterity to incestuous sheets!
>
> Rebellious hell,
> If thou canst mutine in a matron's bones,
> To flaming youth let virtue be as wax
> And melt in her own fire . . .

Grant this, and it still does not excuse his obscenity towards Ophelia —Ophelia whom he had said he loved, and she believed him—and it would not excuse it even if we were to accept Professor Dover

Wilson's shift of a stage direction in II.ii. which makes Hamlet
suspect her as a willing decoy of Claudius and Polonius. What he
says to her in the "get thee to a nunnery" scene and in the play
scene can only be described in D. H. Lawrence's terms as "doing
dirt on sex." But Hamlet was shocked by the revelation of the power
of sex? Yes indeed, as an adolescent may well be horrified and
frightened when the revelation of dangerous powers within comes
as part of a traumatic experience. But Hamlet was not in years an
adolescent; he was, as Shakespeare tells us, a man of thirty. As for
his too vivid picturing of his mother's life with Claudius—

> Not this, by no means, that I bid you do;
> Let the bloat king tempt you again to bed;
> Pinch wanton on your cheek; call you his mouse;
> And let him, for a pair of reechy kisses,
> Or paddling in your neck with his damn'd fingers,
> Make you to ravel all this matter out . . .

—there is enough, here and elsewhere, to give plausibility to the
psychoanalytic speculations of Dr. Ernest Jones.

I am of course aware that what Hamlet says to his mother in the
Closet scene may be regarded as part of a necessary and proper
attempt to break the alliance between her and the smiling murderer;
but through it all runs the impure streak of the indulgence of an
obsessive passion.

> Come, come, and sit you down; you shall not budge;
> You go not till I set you up a glass
> Where you may see the inmost part of you.

If with genuine, even with passionate, concern, you want to help
someone in great need, someone in desperate ignorance of his true
condition, do you, I wonder, say, "This is what you are: see how
ugly you look"? Well, perhaps you may; but certainly not in such
a way that you seem about to make an aggressive attack. The Queen's
immediate reaction, which acts as a stage direction indicating Hamlet's
whole bearing, is, "What wilt thou do? thou wilt not murder me?
Help, help, ho!" Perhaps we may again invoke Lear, who as he
comes to see more and more clearly the evil in the world, is also
constrained to speak words of passionate denunciation: the difference,
from the point of view of our present concern, is that these, like Lear's
"burning shame," have an almost impersonal intensity. Hamlet, in
his denunciations, is never free of himself, never centers entirely on
the matter in hand or the person before him.

Hamlet, in short, is fascinated by what he condemns. His emotions

circle endlessly, but find no direction. And it is because of the im-
purity and indiscriminateness of his rejections that, brief moments
of friendship and respite apart, he takes refuge in postures. There
is a further point to be made here. I do not remember seeing the
question asked, but why, on the success of the Gonzago play, does
Hamlet call for the recorders?

> Ah, ha! Come, some music! come, the recorders!—
> For if the king like not the comedy,
> Why then, belike,—he likes it not, perdy.
> Come, some music!

True, Shakespeare knew that the recorders would be needed for
the scene with Rosencrantz and Guildenstern, but this can hardly
affect the reason imputed to Hamlet. The answer surely can only
be that Hamlet intends the players to finish off the evening with a
concert which Claudius will hear, thus keeping him in suspense and
leaving the initiative of action to him; it will be one more *arranged
scene,* and thus in line with Hamlet's habitual tendency to make
everything, even what he deeply feels, into a matter of playacting.
Again and again intrinsic values, direct relations, are neglected
whilst he tries out various roles before a real or imagined audience.
He dramatizes his melancholy—for he insists on his suit of inky black
even whilst denying its importance—just as he dramatizes his love
and his fall from love and his very grief at Ophelia's death; his jests
and asides imply an approving audience "in the know" and ready to
take the point; he is fascinated by the business of acting (and highly
intelligent about it), and he falls naturally into figures of speech
suggested by the theatre—"make mouths at the invisible event," "Who
calls me villain? breaks my pate across?" etc. Before the last scene
the note of sincerity is found in few places except some of the soliloquies and the intimate exchanges with Horatio.

Now to say that Hamlet adopts histrionic, even at times melo-
dramatic, postures is to bring into view another matter of central
importance—that is, the static quality of Hamlet's consciousness. It
is not for nothing that the popular conception is that this is a play
about delay. Delay in the action, that is in the carrying out of
Hamlet's strategy against the King, can of course be explained: he
had to find out if the Ghost was telling the truth about the murder,
and so on. But the fact remains that one of the most powerful
imaginative effects is of a sense of paralysis. Hamlet feels, and we
are made to feel, that he is "stuck," as we say on more homely
occasions.

> Sure he that made us with such large discourse,
> Looking before and after, gave us not
> That capability and god-like reason
> To fust in us unused. Now, whether it be
> Bestial oblivion, or some craven scruple
> Of thinking too precisely on the event,—
> A thought which, quarter'd, hath but one part wisdom
> And ever three parts coward,—I do not know
> Why yet I live to say "This thing's to do,"
> Sith I have cause, and will, and strength, and means
> To do't.

Hamlet is here of course referring to the specific action of revenge, and commentators have been quick to point out that in regard to outward action he is neither slow nor a coward. But there is another and more important sense in which his self-accusation here is entirely justified, in which he is indeed "lapsed in time and passion"—that is, as Dover Wilson explains, arrested or taken prisoner ("lapsed") by circumstances and passion. Hamlet, as everyone says, is an intellectual, but he does little enough effective thinking on the moral and metaphysical problems that beset him: his god-like reason is clogged and impeded by the emotions of disgust, revulsion and self-contempt that bring him back, again and again, to the isolation of his obsession. Effective thinking, in the regions that most concern Hamlet, implies a capacity for self-forgetfulness and a capacity for true relationship.

With this, I think, we reach the heart of the play. If, as I said earlier in these lectures, in the world of the play there is, on the one hand death, on the other, life lived with a peculiarly crude vigor of self-assertion, in such a world where are values to be found? If we are true to our direct impressions we must admit that *that* is Hamlet's problem, and questions concerning the authenticity of the Ghost or the means whereby Claudius may be trapped are subordinate to it. Hamlet's question, the question that he is continually asking himself, is, How can I live? What shall I do to rid myself of this numbing sense of meaninglessness brought by the knowledge of corruption? But behind this, and implicit in the play as a whole, is the question of being, of the activated consciousness. Hamlet comes close to putting this question directly in the great central soliloquy, but he glides away from it. And no wonder, for the problem is insoluble in the state of unresolved emotion in which he delivers himself of his thoughts; as Coleridge was never tired of insisting, thinking at the higher levels is an activity of the personality as a whole.

Interrogation, Doubt, Irony:

Thesis, Antithesis, Synthesis

by Harry Levin

In reconsidering *Hamlet,* we cannot pretend that we are unaware
of what happens next or how it all comes out. Knowing what will
finally be decided, critics have grown impatient over its agonies of
decision, and have blamed Hamlet for undue procrastination. But
what may be a foregone conclusion to them must be an open question
to him, as we have reminded ourselves by watching the process un-
fold, and observing how the tone is set through the interaction of
questions, answers, and unanswered speculations. Having rehearsed
the play once with an emphasis on the interrogative mood, let us push
the interrogation further by returning to certain indicative passages,
tracing now an inner train of thought, and later placing it in a broader
perspective. *Interrogatio* is classified—by the rhetorician, Henry Pea-
cham—as a form of *pathopoeia,* which in turn is neither more nor
less than a device for arousing emotions: "Examples hereof are common in Tragedies." *Dubitatio,* our next figure of speech and thought,
is less emotional and more deliberative. As it is defined by Abraham
Fraunce, in *The Arcadian Rhetorike,* "Addubitation or doubting is a
kinde of deliberation with our selves." The orator deliberates between rival options: either to revenge or not to revenge, whether a
visitant comes from heaven or hell. For doubt is that state of mind
where the questioner faces no single answer nor the lack of one, but
rather a choice between a pair of alternatives. Etymologically, the
word stems from *dubitare,* which means precisely to hesitate in the
face of two possibilities. The structure of *Hamlet* seems, at every level,

to have been determined by this duality. "A double blessing is a double grace" (I.iii.53).

Similarly, the texture is characterized by a tendency to double and redouble words and phrases. From the very first scene, the speeches abound in hendiadys: "gross and scope," "law and heraldry." Sometimes the paired nouns are redundant synonyms: "food and diet," "pith and moment"—Saxon balancing Latin as in the doublets of Sir Thomas Browne. Adjectives or verbs are coupled at other times: "impotent and bedrid," "countenance and excuse." This reduplication seems to be a habit of courtly diction into which Hamlet himself falls now and then: "the purpose of playing . . . is . . . to show . . . the very age and body of the time his form and pressure" (III.ii.21–5). By the count of R. A. Foakes, no less than 247 such pairings are scattered through the play. They are doubtless more ornamental than functional; yet they charge the air with overtones of wavering and indecision. The Clown goes farther with his equivocations, putting his finger on serious ambiguities. And Hamlet goes too far with his *double entendres,* besmirching the maidenly innocence of Ophelia. Claudius, in his opening address to the Council, establishes himself as a practiced exponent of stately double-talk. With unctuous skill, he manages a transition from the old King's death to himself and his inherited queen. Antithesis is condensed into oxymoron: "delight and dole," "defeated joy." Some of these mannerisms will have their echo in the stilted language of the Play-King: "Grief joys, joy grieves, on slender accident" (III.ii.209). The formal style is a mask, which accords with the dress and etiquette of the court; Claudius is virtually winking, when he speaks of "an auspicious and a dropping eye" (I.ii.11). Hamlet, speaking informally and ironically to Horatio, sums up the paradoxical situation:

> The funeral bak'd meats
> Did coldly furnish forth the marriage tables.

>   (180-81)

The incrimination of Claudius by the Ghost, duly recorded in the book of Hamlet's brain, is an object lesson in duplicity. Claudius himself is unremittingly conscious of the distinction between the "exterior" and "the inward man" (II.ii.6). Both in communing with himself and in dealing with others, he seldom fails to distingush between words and deeds, or face and heart. He introduces Gertrude by publicly casting her in a dual role, "our sometime sister, now our queen," as he does his nephew shortly afterward, "my cousin Hamlet, and my son" (I.ii.8, 64). Hamlet resentfully picks up the implications, and caustically refers to his "uncle-father and aunt-mother" (II.ii.392). On the premise that "man and wife is one flesh," he perversely carries the logic of incest to its conclusion by bidding farewell to Claudius as his "dear mother" (IV.iii.51). He prefaces his interview with Gertrude by resolving to act a part: "My tongue and soul in this be hypocrites" (III.ii.415). He will "speak daggers" to her, and she will admit that his words are "like daggers" (III.iv.95). Addressing her as "your husband's brother's wife," he implores her to keep aloof from Claudius, though she may feel otherwise inclined: "Assume a virtue, if you have it not" (15, 160). It is the recommendation of worldly wisdom that La Rochefoucauld would moralize: "Hypocrisy is the tribute that vice pays to virtue." Molière's *Misanthrope* would reject such sophistications; Alceste stands squarely for virtue disdaining vice; like the ingenuous Hamlet, he knows not "seems." But Hamlet, unlike Alceste, learns to live at court, in an arena where men and women must be actors and actresses. He must learn an etymology which may not have struck him during his humanistic studies at Wittenberg—that the word "hypocrite," in the original Greek, designated an actor.

Claudius, invoking the "twofold force" of prayer, acknowledges his own hypocrisy, caught as he is between guilt and repentance:

> . . . like a man to double business bound,
> I stand in pause where I should first begin.

(III.iii.41-2)

A moment later, Hamlet will stand in pause before the double business of whether Claudius should be saved or damned, and will give him the benefit of an unforeseen doubt. The smiling villain is a double-dealer; but so is Hamlet, in another sense. At the beginning he is single-minded, all of a piece, all melancholia; then he puts on his mask and plays the antic, carrying his buffoonery to the verge of hysteria; his disposition is manic in the presence of others and depressive when he is by himself. Where the vicious Claudius assumes an air of respectability, the virtuous Hamlet must assimilate the atmosphere of licentiousness. He must set aside the high-minded idealism of Castiglione's *Courtier,* "The courtier's, scholar's, soldier's eye, tongue, sword," and take up the time-serving realism of Machiavelli's *Prince* (III.i.159). It is the role of Polonius, as chamberlain, to profess the one and practice the other. While he privately expounds a philosophy of keeping up appearances, he prides himself on his capacity for seeing through them. Master of ceremonies, he bustles about, arranging formalities according to protocol; but he is also a master of palace intrigue, who sneaks behind curtains to spy; and, with him, the play oscillates between ceremonious public hearings and furtive whisperings behind the scenes, so to speak. With the twin figures of Rosencrantz and Guildenstern, the double-dealing is symmetrically personified. Since they invariably hunt in couples, their roles are interchangeable.

Each of them has an introductory speech of exactly the same length
and rhythm, and in each case the key word is "both" (II.ii.26–32).

Thanks, Rosencrantz and gentle Guildenstern,

the King responds, and the Queen preserves the symmetry by adding:

Thanks, Guildenstern and gentle Rosencrantz.

*   *   *

The Gravedigger, who—like so many of Shakespeare's clowns—is an
accomplished dialectician, explains to us that "an act hath three
branches—it is to act, to do, and to perform" (V.i.12–13). This is redundant logic, yet it serves a purpose; it rings the changes on a momentous word, and it comments obliquely on Hamlet's inaction.
Moreover, lest we dally too long before his dilemmas, it reminds us
that the argument must proceed to a third and decisive stage. Our
thesis has been singular, in the person of a solitary being wholly surrounded by questions. Doubts, as to his relations with other beings,
as to the basis of his continued existence, present themselves under
the twofold aspect of an antithesis. These components must be resolved through a synthesis, pieced together out of the playwright's
assumptions about the nature of human experience. The conventional
five-act structure of tragedy is ignored by the Quartos of *Hamlet,* indicated for only the first two acts of the Folio text, and completed by
later editors. Granville-Barker's recommendation, which best accords
with modern theatrical usage, is that we conceive the play as a work
composed in three movements. "Treble woe" is the fatality that over-
takes Polonius and his two children. Threefold also are the consequences of the original sin against the old King, his loss "Of life, of
crown, of queen" (I.v.75). The drama might almost be described as
a triangle play with a vengeance. The interrelationship of Hamlet
the Elder, Claudius, and Gertrude predominates in the mind of Hamlet the Younger. Perhaps it has some bearing upon his tendency to
triple his phrases: "O, horrible! O, horrible! most horrible!" (I.v.80).
"Words, words, words" (II.ii.194). "Mother, mother, mother!" (III.iv.6).

Our third trope, *ironia,* is more than a figure of speech or even of
thought; it may be a point of view, a view of life, and—as such—a
resolvent for contrarieties. Its most clear-cut form, designated in Put-
tenham's *Arte of English Poesie* as "the drye mock," is a statement
which means the contrary of what it purports to say. Caesar was ambitious; Brutus was honorable; yet Antony contrives, by his mocking
inflection, to carry the opposite impression in both regards. Dubious
statements could be reversed by simply adding the Elizabethan inter-
jection *quotha.* Hamlet makes the controversion explicit, when his
mother asks him, "What shall I do?" (III.iv.180). He has just told her,

directly, "go not to my uncle's bed." Now he elaborates, "Not this, by
no means, that I bid you do." In other words, what follows is to be
taken ironically: "Let the bloat King tempt you again to bed . . ."
And Hamlet dwells, with ambivalent detail, on the endearments he
would have her avoid. Given the hypocrisy of the court, where one
may not say what one means, honesty must either hold its tongue or
express itself through indirection. When Polonius begs to take his
leave, Hamlet's tone of politeness thinly disguises his eagerness to
confer the favor begged: "You cannot, sir, take from me anything
that I will more willingly part withal—" Whereupon his dry mock
deepens into a thrice-uttered heartcry: "except my life, except my life,
except my life" (II.ii.217–21). To the initial queries of Claudius and
Gertrude, his hedging answers are verbal ironies. Gertrude's naïve
reaction to the Play-Queen—"The lady doth protest too much, me-
thinks"—unconsciously lays bare her own standards of conduct. Hamlet's double-edged comment, "O, but she'll keep her word," is ostensi-
bly another bit of polite conversation (III.ii.240–41). Actually, he is
distorting the play-within-the-play in order to drive home an invidi-
ous contrast. The Play-Queen will have no chance to keep her word;
the Queen of Denmark had a chance and failed.

As for the King, his usual mode is merely hypocritical; but, under
the goading of Hamlet, he too waxes ironic. When he announces the
excursion to England, and Hamlet assents with "Good," Claudius
says, "So is it, if thou knew'st our purposes" (IV.iii.48–9). He is having
his grim little joke, and assuming Hamlet is unaware that what might
be good for Claudius would not be good for himself. But the joke is
on Claudius; for he does not know that Hamlet knows his purposes,
that he himself is rather a step behind than a step ahead of his oppo-
nent. Hamlet's retort is enigmatic, if not ironic, with its cryptic allusion to the Ghost: "I see a cherub that sees them." The irony now
lies not in the statement but in the situation, which will turn out to
be the contrary of what Claudius designs. Hamlet has already ventured a prediction, in his farewell to his mother. There, in hinting at
the treachery of Rosencrantz and Guildenstern, whom he will trust as
he would "adders fang'd," he has defined the process of dramatic irony:

> For 'tis the sport to have the engineer
> Hoist with his own petar.

> (III.iv.203, 206-7)

It is always exciting when craft meets equal craftiness in a battle of
wits. But there is peculiar satisfaction in watching, when vaunted
cleverness overreaches itself. The comic formula of the cheater
cheated, *Wily Beguiled,* is transmuted into the imagery of siege and
explosion, as Hamlet conspires with himself to blow his enemies at

the moon. The actual conspiracy, when it happens, will be literary rather than military; it will consist of forging a royal mandate, so that Rosencrantz and Guildenstern will be executed in Hamlet's place; and this will be retrospectively disclosed by Hamlet to Horatio, with rhetorical flourishes parodying the style of Claudius. Thus the episode has been somewhat glossed over, particularly the incidental deaths of the schoolfellows; but it had been a conspicuous feature of the primitive legend; and its elements, widely diffused in folklore, persist through the *motif* of a lucky youth with an ill-fated letter. Hamlet's prototype is the unsuspecting hero, sent on a journey bearing his own death warrant; jolted into some realization of the hazards confronting him, he finally turns adversity into advantage.

Another element in the archaic tale has proved susceptible of endless refinement. This was the spectacle of a cunning hero forced to wear a mask of stupidity, which originally lent Hamlet his oafish name. In dissembling, in counterfeiting madness, in playing his antic part, he exemplifies the humanistic tradition of the wise fool. In his wayward fashion, he pursues the wisdom of Socrates, which characteristically masqueraded as ignorance. Hamlet's behavior has been characterized by a student of Shakespeare's wit and humor, John Weiss, as a "sustained gesture of irony." It is that gesture which enables the questioner to reject seeming for being, which helps the doubter to distinguish between appearance and reality. In the dual role of an ironist, Hamlet can remain his tragic self while presenting a quasi-comic front. The dissembler of Aristophanic comedy, the *eiron,* had shrewdly exposed the impostor or *alazon.* Neoclassicists like Voltaire were historically warranted in associating the ironic with the comic and deeming it inappropriate for tragedy. The concept was broadly extended by Bishop Thirlwall's essay "On the Irony of Sophocles." If the Greek tragedians had been ironists, it was not because they mocked at their fellow men, but because they concerned themselves with the mockery of fate. Oedipus is the engineer of his own downfall; and his blinding is a requital for taunting the blind Tiresias, as well as an expiation of his trespasses. Human agency seems to confound itself through the workings of some cosmic design. So it seems to the Play-King:

> Our wills and fates do so contrary run
> That our devices still are overthrown.

(III.ii.221-2)

That overthrow is made ironic by the perception of counterdevices, by the aptness with which fates are matched against wills. The outcome must belie the expectation, the disappointment must become concrete, through some logical connection or personal association.

This correspondence between device and counterdevice takes its most obvious form in the equivocal oracle. The riddling prophecies that cajole and betray Macbeth are the merest plays upon words, which are carried out by charades on the part of Birnam Wood and Macduff. In *King Lear* the irony is classical when the gods are said to have justly taken Cornwall's life for Gloucester's sight; it is more problematic when Gloucester accuses them of treating mortals as wanton boys treat flies. Poetic justice, which prevails in *Macbeth,* miscarries in *King Lear,* where the ways of providence are as unfathomable as in *Hamlet.*

With *Hamlet,* as we have seen, we are involved in two sets of complementary problems. One set is speculative: why? wherefore? who is the Ghost? and what is the ultimate mystery that it prefigures? The other is practical: what shall we do? how should Hamlet bear himself amid these unexampled difficulties? and how should he accomplish his unsought vocation, revenge? Shakespearean tragedy is deeply concerned with the individual as he faces opportunity, responsibility, and moral choice. It is equally preoccupied with the pattern of events, and whether this is determined by casual accident, fatal necessity, or divine intervention. Given the motive, one must await one's cue. The interplay between these preoccupations is the source of innumerable ironies, both conscious and unconscious, some of them attached to the hero's viewpoint, others detached in a reminiscent overview. "Hamlet has no plan, but *Hamlet* has," as Goethe observed, with a fellow dramatist's understanding. The play has a plot; and so, in another sense, has the Prince; but he cannot foresee the fulfilment of his intentions; he can only test them against hugger-mugger conditions. Yet, as producer of "The Murder of Gonzago," he can take charge of a miniature drama which exerts an effect on the drama at large; he can play god and look down on his creation, in the self-conscious mood of romantic irony. Whereas in *Hamlet* itself, he is no more than a leading actor, whose body will be placed "on a stage" —on a funeral bier which may likewise be viewed as a theatrical platform—among the other corpses at the end. It will then become Horatio's function to play the commentator, and to report upon the ironic upshot of the whole story: "purposes mistook/Fall'n on th' inventors' heads" (V.ii.389, 395–6).

Hamlet points the analogy himself when he addresses the surviving onlookers as "audience to this act" (346). The verb "to act" is synonymous with "to do," in the patient explanation of the Gravedigger, but also with the ambiguous "to perform." "The name of action" has further branches for Hamlet; it often takes on this theatrical inflection, as when he declares that the customs of mourning are "actions that a man might play" (I.ii.84). Conversely, he is pleading for sincer-

ity, when he tells the Players: "Suit the action to the word, the word
to the action" (III.ii.19–20). The noun "act" conveys a sexual innu-
endo, when it is bandied back and forth between Hamlet and Gertrude in the Closet Scene. Some of these ambiguities might be clarified
in the light of God's law, if not of man's; for above us "the action
lies/In his true nature," as Claudius confesses to himself (III.iii.61–2).
Here below, deeds may be obfuscated by words, as they have been in
his own case; or else they may be retarded by thoughts, as they are
in Hamlet's.

> I do not know
> Why yet I live to say "This thing's to do,"
> Sith I have cause, and will, and strength, and means
> To do't.
>
> (IV.iv.43-6)

Again and again he reproaches himself in this tone; but self-reproach
is a sign of conscientiousness rather than cowardice. The Ghost reappears, at an awkward moment, to whet Hamlet's "almost blunted
purpose"; but ghosts, after all, are notorious for nagging, especially
on the Elizabethan stage (III.iv.111). It takes no less than five of them
to rouse Chapman's Senecal hero to *The Revenge of Bussy D'Ambois;*
and yet his bravery is widely and loudly attested. Because we are
privileged to overhear Hamlet's moments of self-questioning, or to
glimpse his incertitude before psychic phenomena, we should not
make the mistake of considering him a weak or passive figure. That
his native disposition is active and resolute, though it has been tem-
porarily sicklied over with the pale cast of melancholy—such an impression is fully confirmed by objective testimony from the other
characters. *"Hamlet* is not a drama of weakness," its Russian translator, Boris Pasternak, has clairvoyantly noted, "but of duty and self-
denial."

The critical sentimentalization of Hamlet's personality has leaned
heavily on the expression, *Gedankenschauspiel,* wrenched from its
context in A. W. Schlegel's lectures and mistranslated as "tragedy of
thought." This has encouraged the obscurantist conclusion that
thought is Hamlet's tragedy; Hamlet is the man who thinks too
much, ineffectual because he is intellectual; his nemesis is a failure
of nerve, a nervous prostration. Schlegel wanted merely to underline
the well-taken point that *Hamlet* was, above all, a drama of ideas,
a dramatization of man's intellectual curiosity. By the canons of the
humanists, the highest virtue was knowledge put into action. But
how to know what to do? That was the question; there was the rub.
Hamlet's plight is magnified by the tension between the stream of
his highly skeptical consciousness and the undercurrents of murky

superstition and swirling paganism. Hence he stands as the very arche-
type of character at odds with destiny, of the incompatibility between
will and fate.

*   *   *

There may be other Shakespearean characters who are just as memo-
rable, and other plots which are no less impressive; but nowhere else
has the outlook of the individual in a dilemma been so profoundly
realized; and a dilemma, by definition, is an all but unresolvable
choice between evils. Rather than with calculation or casuistry, it
should be met with the virtue of readiness; sooner or later it will
have to be grasped by one or the other of its horns. These, in their
broadest terms, have been—for Hamlet, as we interpret him—the
problem of what to believe and the problem of how to act. Hamlet
is unwittingly compelled to act as if life were a duel, with unbated
swords and against a series of furtive assailants. He is unwillingly led
to believe that death comes as a cup, filled with poisonous wine and
containing a flawless pearl. His doom is generalized in Fulke Gre-
ville's chorus:

> Oh, wearisome condition of humanity,
> Born under one law, to another bound . . .

Irony cannot solve the incalculable contradictions between the personal life and the nature of things. Yet it can teach us to live with
them; and that is no mean achievement; for Hamlet's knowledge was
not idle reflection, according to Nietzsche. It was an insight which
hindered action by stripping the veil of illusion from the terrible
truth, the terror or the absurdity of existence. This would be intoler-
able, were it not for the transformations of art, which asserts man's
conquest over his fears, and which thereby allays his vexation of spirit.
Thus Hamlet's limited victory commences with the play-within-the-
play, a working model of the play itself, which repeats the lesson in
mastery on a larger scale within our minds. From its very commence-
ment, after the stroke of midnight, we are brought face to face with
the supernatural. Volleys of gunfire augment and accelerate the sound
effects until, at the conclusion of the dead march, *"a peal of ord-
nance"* signalizes a battle lost and won.

Hamlet as Minister and Scourge

by Fredson Bowers

When Hamlet is first preparing to leave his mother's chamber after harrowing her to repentance, he turns to the dead body of Polonius:

> For this same lord,
> I do repent; but heaven hath pleas'd it so,
> To punish me with this, and this with me,
> That I must be their scourge and minister.
> I will bestow him, and will answer well
> The death I gave him.
>
> (III.iv.172-177)

These provocative, if not enigmatic, lines have received comparatively small attention. In my opinion they contain perhaps the clearest analysis Hamlet makes of his predicament, and are therefore worth a scrupulous enquiry.

The Variorum quotes Malone's paraphrase, "To punish me by making me the instrument of this man's death, and to punish this man by my hand." This is surely the literal meaning of the first lines. Going beyond Malone by seeking the nature of Hamlet's punishment, both Dover Wilson and Kittredge agree that "To punish me with this" means, substantially, that Hamlet perceives his secret will be revealed to Claudius, with serious consequences to himself. Kittredge writes, "the King will at once perceive that he killed Polonius by mistake for him, and will take measures accordingly." And Dover Wilson (quoting "This man shall set me packing"): "The death of Polonius has placed Hamlet within the power of the King."

This view is only superficially plausible, and it should not satisfy as offering the complete, or even the true, interpretation. The reason for Heaven's punishment is left unexamined, and no account is taken of the close syntactical relationship between the first statement about the double punishment, and the second, "That I must be their [i.e., Heaven's] scourge and minister."

"Hamlet as Minister and Scourge" by Fredson Bowers. From Publications of the Modern Language Association, LXX (1955), 740-749. Copyright © 1955 by the Modern Language Association. Reprinted by permission of the author and PMLA.

For a moment let us look at this second statement. Kittredge comes near to the meaning: "heaven's scourge (of punishment) and heaven's agent—minister of divine retribution." This implies a difference between a scourge and a minister, that is, between an instrument of punishment and one of divine retribution; but how retribution differs from punishment is not indicated, nor is the question considered why Hamlet describes himself in both capacities.

In cases of doubt it is always well to work back through the text. "For this same lord, I do repent." In spite of whatever callousness Hamlet exhibits in "Thou wretched, rash, intruding fool, farewell!" and in "I'll lug the guts into the neighbour room," or in "Safely stow'd," his stated repentance must be based on more than merely practical considerations that now the hunt will be up. Although Polonius' folly has been punished by Hamlet, yet an innocent man has been killed, and Hamlet has stained his hands with blood without attaining his main objective. His attempt at revenge has led him to commit a murder which he had never contemplated. A modern audience is less likely to feel the horror of Polonius' death than an Elizabethan, which would have known from the moment the rapier flashed through the arras that Hamlet was thereafter a doomed man. On the Elizabethan stage, blood demanded blood; and at the most only two or three tragic characters who draw blood for private motives survive the denouement, and then only at the expense of a retirement to the cloister for the rest of their lives.[1]

Hamlet, no bloody madman, may well repent that he has killed an innocent person. This mistake does not excuse him. Elizabethan law, like ours, was very clear that if by premeditation one kills, but accidentally mistakes the object and slays the wrong man, the case was still premeditated murder in the first degree, not manslaughter.[2]

Hamlet repents at the personal level, yet adds, "but heaven hath pleas'd it so,/To punish me with this." There are two implications here. First, Hamlet recognizes that his repentance cannot wash the blood from his hands, and that he must accept whatever penalty is in store for him. Second, the "this" with which he is punished is certainly the body of Polonius, and thus the fact of murder, carrying with it the inevitable penalty for blood. To view heaven's punishment as no more than the exposure of Hamlet's intents to Claudius, so that the revenge will thereafter be made more difficult, is a shallow concept which ignores the blood that has just been shed in defiance of divine law. I am concerned that the primary implication be made clear: Hamlet feels that it has pleased Heaven to punish him with the

---

[1] As in Marston's *Antonio's Revenge* and Fletcher's *Bloody Brother*. See also my *Elizabethan Revenge Tragedy* (Princeton Univ. Press, 1940), pp. 11-12, 39-40.

[2] *Elizabethan Revenge Tragedy*, p. 9.

central fact of murder and one that bore no relation to his mission of justice; moreover, that he has killed the wrong man is an essential part of this punishment.

If Heaven's punishment is taken merely as the revelation of Hamlet's secret to Claudius, with all the consequences that are sure to follow, the punishment would have been comparatively mild, for the play-within-a-play had already effectively revealed Hamlet to Claudius, as well as Claudius to Hamlet. If we carefully follow the implications of the action within the setting of the time-scheme, it is clear that immediately following the mousetrap, and before the killing of Polonius, Claudius has seen Hamlet's murderous intents and has set on foot a plot to kill him. When first conceived after the eavesdropping on Hamlet and Ophelia in the nunnery scene, the English voyage was an innocent expedient to get a peculiarly behaving Hamlet out of the country, perhaps to his cure. However, it becomes a murderous scheme immediately after the play-within-a-play when Claudius changes the ceremonious details and plans to send Hamlet away in the same ship with Rosencrantz and Guildenstern, a necessary factor for the altered commission ordering Hamlet's execution in England. No hint is given that Claudius has altered the original commission in the short interval between the Queen's announcement of Polonius' death and the appearance of Hamlet before him for questioning, nor would there have been time. We learn only that Polonius' death must expedite Hamlet's departure; and hence we are required to assume that the discussion of the commission immediately following the mousetrap play involved what we later learn to have been the important change commanding Hamlet's death. Viewed in this light, the dead body of Polonius cannot punish Hamlet by revealing his secret to Claudius, for that has previously been revealed, and Claudius has already set on foot a lethal plot to dispose of his stepson.

Of course, Hamlet does not know of the change in the purport of the commission, it might be argued. But it would be most difficult to argue that Hamlet was not quite aware that in stripping the truth from Claudius by the doctored-up *Murder of Gonzago,* he had simultaneously revealed himself. The circumstances and language of the play were too damning for him to think that more than the façade of pretense could stand between him and Claudius after that episode. Hence I take it that the conventional interpretation of Hamlet's words ignores their deeper religious significance, and offers only a meaningless redundancy as a substitute.

> but heaven hath pleas'd it so,
> To punish me with this, and this with me,
> That I must be their scourge and minister.

We may paraphrase thus: Heaven has contrived this killing as a means of punishing us both and as a means of indicating to me that I must be its scourge and minister.

One need only dig down to this bare meaning to reveal how little the basic ideas have really been explained. Three difficult questions immediately assert themselves. Why was Heaven punishing Hamlet by making him the instrument of Polonius' death? Why does this punishment place him in the position of scourge and minister? What is the difference, if any, between scourge and minister? These are best answered, perhaps, in inverse order. The standard religious concept of the time was that God intervened in human affairs in two ways, internally and externally. Internally, God could punish sin by arousing the conscience of an individual to a sense of grief and remorse, which might in extraordinary cases grow so acute as to lead to madness. Externally, God worked through inanimate, or at least subhuman objects, through the forces of Nature, and through the agency of human beings. God's vengeance might strike a criminal by causing a sudden and abnormal mortal sickness, by sinking him in a squall at sea, by hitting him over the head with a falling timber, by leading him accidentally into a deep quicksand or unseen pool. The Elizabethans, if there was any suspected reason, were inclined to see God's hand in most such accidents. But sometimes Heaven punished crime by human agents, and it was standard belief that for this purpose God chose for His instruments those who were already so steeped in crime as to be past salvation. This was not only a principle of economy, but a means of freeing God from the impossible assumption that He would deliberately corrupt innocence. When a human agent was selected to be the instrument of God's vengeance, and the act of vengeance on the guilty necessitated the performance by the agent of a crime, like murder, only a man already damned for his sins was selected, and he was called a scourge.[3]

Any man who knew himself to be such a scourge knew both his function and his fate: his powers were not his own. Taking the long view, no matter how much he could glory in the triumphs of the present, his position was not an enviable one. Any human agent used by God to visit wrath and to scourge evil by evil was already condemned. This idea is clearly stated at the end of Fletcher's *Maid's Tragedy:*

> on lustful kings
> Unlook'd-for sudden deaths from God are sent;
> But curs'd is he that is their instrument.

[3] Roy Battenhouse, *Marlowe's "Tamburlaine"* (Vanderbilt Univ. Press, 1941), pp. 13-15, 108-113.

When Hamlet called himself a scourge of Heaven, it is inconceivable that the Elizabethan audience did not know what he meant, and that Hamlet did not realize to the full what he was saying.

Although some writers, as in Fortescue's translation *The Forest*,[4] used scourge and minister interchangeably, there was a general tendency to distinguish them. The references in the concordance show, for our purposes, that Shakespeare always means minister in a good sense unless he specifies that the minister is of hell. A minister of God, in contrast to a scourge, is an agent who directly performs some good. In this sense, heavenly spirits are ministers of grace, as Hamlet calls them. The good performed by a human minister, however, may be some positive good in neutral or in good circumstances, or it may be some good which acts as a direct retribution for evil by overthrowing it and setting up a positive good in its place. The distinction between minister and scourge, thus, lies in two respects. First, a retributive minister may visit God's wrath on sin but only as the necessary final act to the overthrow of evil, whereas a scourge visits wrath alone, the delayed good to rest in another's hands. To take a rough and ready example, Richard III was thought of as a scourge for England, the final agent of God's vengeance for the deposition and murder of the anointed Richard II; but the good wishes of the ghosts make young Henry Richmond, in Raleigh's description, "the immediate instrument of God's justice," that is, a minister who will bring to a close God's wrath by exacting public justice in battle on the tyrant Richard, this triumph to be followed by a reign of peace and glory under the Tudor dynasty. In the second respect, as a contrast to the evil and damned scourge, if a minister's duty is to exact God's punishment or retribution as an act of good, his hands will not be stained with crime. If in some sense he is the cause of the criminal's death, the means provided him by Heaven will lie in some act of public justice, or of vengeance, rather than in criminal private revenge.

We are now in a position to examine Hamlet's "scourge and minister." We must recognize that the Ghost's command, though not explicit, was at first interpreted by Hamlet as a call to an act of private blood-revenge. Yet there is no getting around the fact that to an Elizabethan audience this was a criminal act of blood, not to be condoned by God, and therefore represented a particularly agonizing position for a tragic hero to be placed in. If Hamlet hopes to right the wrong done him and his father, and to ascend the throne of Denmark with honor, he must contrive a public vengeance which will demonstrate him to be a minister of Heaven's justice. Yet the secret murder of his father, so far as he can see, prevents all hope of public

---

4 See Battenhouse, p. 13, for a typical quotation.

justice; and therefore the circumstances appear to him to enforce a criminal private revenge even after he realizes that he has been supernaturally appointed as a minister. The enormous contrast between Hamlet's first promise to sweep to his revenge and his concluding, "The time is out of joint. O cursed spite,/That ever I was born to set it right," has often been remarked, but not sufficiently against this background. Moreover, it has not been well considered that if the Ghost is a spirit of health, it could not escape from purgatory under its own volition in order to influence affairs on earth. Since divine permission alone could free the Ghost to revisit the earth, the Ghost's demand for the external punishment of Claudius, and its prophecy of the internal punishment of Gertrude, is not alone a personal call but in effect the transmission of a divine command, appointing Hamlet as God's agent to punish the specific criminal, Claudius.

With the final line of *The Maid's Tragedy* in our ears—"But curs'd is he that is their instrument"—we may see with full force the anomalous position Hamlet conceives for himself: is he to be the private-revenger scourge *or* the public-revenger minister? If scourge, he will make his own opportunities, will revenge murder with murder, and by this means visit God's wrath on corruption. If minister, God will see to it that a proper opportunity is offered in some way that will keep him clear from crime, one which will preserve him to initiate a good rule over Denmark. This crux for Hamlet has not been really pointed up, in part because Shakespeare had no need to make it explicit for his own audience.

As a consequence, Hamlet at the start finds himself in this peculiarly depressing position. He has been set aside from other human beings as an agent of God to set right the disjointed times, and he may reasonably assume from the circumstances of the ghostly visitation that he is a minister. Every private emotion urges him to a personal revenge of blood as the only means of solving his problem, and this revenge seems enforced by the secrecy of the original crime. But if he acts thus, he will be anticipating God's will, which in its good time will provide the just opportunity. If he anticipates and revenges, he risks damnation. If he does not revenge, he must torture himself with his seeming incompetence. In moments of the deepest depression, it could be natural for doubts to arise as to his role, and whether because of his "too too sullied flesh" he may not in fact have been appointed as a scourge, in which case his delay is indeed cowardly. Finally, there arises the important doubt whether the Ghost has been a demon to delude him into damning his soul by the murder of an innocent man, or indeed an agent of Heaven appointing him to an act of justice.

With these considerations in mind, the two months' delay between

the Ghost's visitation and the next appearance of Hamlet in Act II
may seem to have more validity than certain rather bloodthirsty critics
will allow. I suggest that this delay, which Shakespeare never explicitly motivates, was caused not alone by rising doubts of the Ghost, or
by the physical difficulties of getting at Claudius, or by the repugnance of a sensitive young man to commit an act of murder, or by his
examining the circumstances so over-scrupulously as to become lost
in the mazes of thought, motive, and doubt; but instead as much as
anything by Hamlet as minister waiting on the expected opportunity
which should be provided him, and not finding it.[5] The strain is, of
course, tremendous, and it gives rise not only to his depressed musing
on life and death in "To be or not to be" but also to the self-castiga-
tion of "O what a rogue and peasant slave." The corruption of the
world, of men and women, and of Denmark with its interfering Polonius, its complaisant Ophelia, its traitorous Rosencrantz and Guildenstern whose love has been bought away from their schoolfellow—but
especially of Denmark's source of corruption, its murderer-King and
lustful, incestuous Queen—seem to cry out for scourging. To satisfy
at least one question, he contrives the mousetrap and secures his answer, in the process revealing himself. And immediately an opportunity is given him for private revenge in the prayer scene, but one
so far different from divinely appointed public vengeance that Heaven
would never have provided it for its minister, a sign that the time
is not yet. He passes on, racking himself with blood-thirsty promises,
and—no longer trusting to Heaven's delays—impulsively takes the next
action upon himself. He kills Polonius, thinking him the King. He
repents, but does not expect his repentance to alter the scales of justice. Heaven, it is clear, has punished him for anticipating by his
own deed the opportunity that was designed for the future. The
precise form of the punishment consists in the fact that in killing, he
has slain the wrong man; and the fact that it was Polonius and not
the King behind the arras is the evidence for Heaven's punishment.
He has irretrievably stained his hands with innocent blood by his
usurping action, and foreseeing Heaven withheld his proper victim
as its punishment.[6]

[5] Strongly corroborative is the evidence of Tourneur's *Atheist's Tragedy,* a play
manifestly influenced by *Hamlet* and one which carries this situation to its logical
conclusion.

[6] That Heaven was behind all acts of reward or punishment is so much an article
of Elizabethan tragic doctrine as to be instantly accepted at its face value by the
audience without scrupulous enquiry into the hidden workings by which Heaven
produced the results. Nor is it likely **that** Shakespeare worried much about the exact
method or implications of this working in the situation in question. Heaven could
readily order the ironic accident which, as a punishment, placed Polonius rather
than Claudius behind the arras. However, with the proviso that there is no need to

As I interpret it, therefore, Hamlet is not only punished *for* the murder of Polonius but *with* his murder, since Polonius was not his assigned victim; hence this fact is the evidence for Heaven's displeasure at his private revenge. The punishment *for* the murder will come, as indeed it does: it is this incident which for the Elizabethan audience motivated the justice of the tragic catastrophe and makes the closet scene the climax of the play.[7] Hamlet's words show his own

---

believe that Shakespeare or his audience sought out the implications in full detail, it may be remarked that the action of Heaven was theologically explicable. The crucial point is the distinction between foreknowledge and fore-ordination. It cannot be taken that Heaven fore-ordained that Hamlet should disobey and impulsively attempt revenge before Heaven had provided the opportunity and means for exhibiting the act as one of justice. On the other hand, one cannot limit the knowledge of God; and thus Heaven could foresee that Hamlet would perform this action. Conditional upon this foreknowledge, therefore, Heaven orders it so that Polonius substitutes for Claudius. The actions of Heaven conditional upon God's knowledge of the future are theologically quite different from Heaven's preordination, which wills certain events to take place.

7 This point needs emphasis because the prayer scene is still occasionally cited as the climax. The climax is that scene in a play in which an action occurs which tips the scales for or against the fate of the protagonist in terms of the future action. The arguments for the prayer scene as the climax are superficial, for they turn only on the point that Hamlet suffers death in the catastrophe because he spared Claudius in this scene. Two considerations are always present in a tragedy. First, the climax must directly produce a train of action that leads to the catastrophe. Second, if we may briefly define tragedy as a series of morally determinate actions, the climactic scene must involve a morally determined action which justifies the tragic catastrophe to come. If we survey the prayer scene according to these two considerations, we may see that neither applies. Plotwise, no train of action results from the sparing of Claudius. Claudius' own plan, the English voyage with its deadly ending, has already been set in motion, but is to prove abortive. On the contrary, as a direct result of the killing of Polonius the plot picks up Laertes as his revenger. Claudius' own plan of the poisoned cup backfires and is one of the means for his downfall, but Laertes' plan succeeds and is the immediate cause of Hamlet's death. By a direct and continuous line of action the catastrophe goes back to the killing of Polonius. What the action of the play would have been like if Laertes had not had the occasion to revenge the death of his father, we cannot tell. This in itself is enough to remove the prayer scene from consideration as the climax from the point of view of the plot. As for the second requirement—the morally determinate action—if Hamlet's sparing of Claudius is to be a tragic error of such magnitude as to make his subsequent death an act of justice, we must take it that he should have killed Claudius at prayer. This would require the audience to be convinced that Hamlet's decision was wrong in the light of his belief that Claudius was in a state of grace. It is difficult to see how such a theory could be defended. On the other hand, if the ethical climax is to coincide with the plot climax, as it should, we are forced into examining the killing of Polonius as a morally determined action. Greek tragedy might have made of this scene a study of simple fatal error, something like Oedipus slaying his father, and drawn the moral of the ways in which fate interferes with human life. But the Elizabethan is not the Greek drama, and the English tragic writers would have agreed with Milton's God who pronounces, "What I will is Fate." The general Christian framework of Elizabethan tragic ethics demands that the slaying of

recognition that he has in part made himself a scourge by the mistaken murder; and I suggest that it is his acceptance of this part of his total role that leads him to send Rosencrantz and Guildenstern so cheerfully, at least on the surface, to their doom. In his mind they are of the essence of the court's corruption under Claudius. They are adders fanged.

When next we see Hamlet, after the interlude of the graveyard scene, a manifest change has taken place. When he left for England, as shown by his "How all occasions do inform against me" soliloquy, he was still torn by his earlier dilemma of somehow reconciling the combat of his private emotions for revengeful action against the restraint of waiting on divine will. But it appears to him that very shortly Heaven reversed its course and actively demonstrated its guidance by preserving his life from the King's plot and returning him to Denmark, short-circuiting the delay of an English adventure. The conflict has certainly been resolved, and it is a different Hamlet indeed who tells Horatio that "There's a divinity that shapes our ends,/ Rough-hew them how we will." He directly imputes his unsealing of the commission to heavenly prompting, and Heaven was even ordinant in providing him with his father's signet to reseal the papers. The pirates, it is clear, were only the natural culmination of Heaven's intervention on his side to bring him back to Denmark for the long-withheld vengeance.

When he recapitulates his wrongs, a new and quite different item is appended. It is true that Claudius, as he says, has killed his father, whored his mother, popped in between the election and his hopes, and has even attempted Hamlet's life by treacherous device. He demands for these, "Is't not perfect conscience/To quit him with this arm?" And then, significantly, he adds, "And is't not to be damn'd/ To let this canker of our nature come/To further evil?" This is a note not heard before, an argument which would be used not by a private revenger but by one seeking public vengeance and justice. It says in effect: knowing what I know now, especially in this attempt on my life, I should be an accessory before the fact, and thus equally guilty

---

Polonius be more than an unlucky accident. So far as I can see, the only way to give it a moral determinism is to argue, as I do, that it was a real error for Hamlet to attempt his private revenge at this time when Heaven had put him in a position of a minister for whom public justice would be arranged at Heaven's own pleasure. The tragic error consists in the fact that Hamlet's emotional drive is too strong to permit him to wait upon what appears to him to be Heaven's extraordinary delay. Paradoxically, therefore, the tragic fact is not Hamlet's delay except for its effect upon his cumulative impatience, but instead his attempt at action. Once again, Tourneur's *Atheist's Tragedy* must be cited, with its protagonist who is in the same fix but who successfully overcomes the temptation to anticipate Heaven and who therefore survives.

with Claudius, if by further delay I permit him to enact more crimes. I should be directly responsible for further evil effects, and therefore I must see that his crimes are stopped.

Shakespeare here, as elsewhere, gives Hamlet no precise plan. But the note of confidence, not hitherto heard, is of the utmost importance. Before, when the ways of God were not at all apparent to his mind, we had "O what a rogue and peasant slave," or "How all occasions do inform against me." Now he says to Horatio, "The interim is mine," serene in trust that divine providence will guide him. Critics have noted this end to self-recrimination and conflict but have thought it odd that his confidence was based on no definite plan of action. Properly viewed, that is the precise point and it is one of great importance. His lack of plan and thus his insistence on providence arises from his confidence in Heaven. This is not lip-service or religious commonplace, but the very heart of the matter.

Immediately, Claudius' counterplot begins and the fencing match is arranged. Hamlet's assured feeling that he is only an instrument in the hands of God sustains him against the ominous portent of disaster that seizes on his heart. For he has learned his lesson from the results of killing Polonius. "There's a special providence in the fall of a sparrow," he says to Horatio; "if it be not now, yet it will come"; and, finally, the summation, "The readiness is all."

From the Elizabethan point of view, divine providence works out the catastrophe with justice. The plotters are hoist by their own villainous schemes; and then, triumphantly, the opportunity is given Hamlet to kill Claudius in circumstances which relieve him from immortal penalty for blood. By stage doctrine he must die for the slaying of Polonius, and, more doubtfully, for that of Rosencrantz and Guildenstern perhaps, the first in which he was inadvertently and the second consciously a scourge; and that penalty is being exacted. Since he cannot now ascend the throne over Claudius' body, all possible self-interest is removed. He has not plotted Claudius' death in cold blood, but seized an opportunity which under no circumstances he could have contrived by blood-revenge, to kill as a dying act of public justice a manifest and open murderer, exposed by the death of Gertrude, while himself suffering the pangs of death as his victim. The restitution of right lies only in him. Despite the terrible action of his forcing the poisoned cup between the King's teeth, Shakespeare takes great pains to remove the blood guilt from Hamlet by the expiation of his own death, and to indicate that the open killing was a ministerial act of public justice accomplished under the only possible circumstances. Hamlet's death is sufficient to expiate that of Polonius in the past and of Laertes in the present. With Christian charity Hamlet accepts Laertes' repentance and forgiveness accompanied by

the prayer that "Mine and my father's death come not upon thee"
in the future life; and in turn he prays that Heaven will make Laertes
free from the guilt of his own. Finally, Horatio's blessing, "Flights of
angels sing thee to thy rest," are words of benediction for a minister
of providence who died through anticipating heavenly justice but,
like Samson, was never wholly cast off for his tragic fault and in the
end was honored by fulfilling divine plan in expiatory death. In more
ways than one, but not necessarily more than he meant by his prophecy, Hamlet kept his promise for Polonius, "I will answer well the
death I gave him."

The Theme

by Bertram Joseph

To imagine *Hamlet* in detail is to imagine a world in which the murderer, Claudius, succeeds in establishing himself as an acceptable substitute for his victim, his dead brother, whose widow and subjects are soon corrupted into embracing the evil which presents itself as good. Nevertheless, Claudius is maneuvered into betraying his guilt to two pairs of eyes (though he never realizes that Horatio as well as Hamlet shares his secret). From then on he plans deliberately to destroy his nephew, even poisoning the wine in public when Laertes loses the first bout. Claudius manages to destroy Hamlet, but only at the cost of his own life, and of exposing his own treachery in this instance, leaving Horatio to give an account of the full villainy:

> Even while men's minds are wild, lest more mischance
> On plots and errors happen.
>
> (V.ii.386-7)

Claudius' success in substituting himself for his brother is accurately described when Hamlet calls the world an unweeded garden, adding:

> things rank and gross in nature
> Possess it merely.
>
> (I.ii.136-7)

To possess something *merely* does not mean simply to own it completely; *mere possession* is the Elizabethan term for squatters' rights. Claudius is established in his brother's place for the want of anybody's having taken the trouble to dispute his right of possession.

Rank is the word Hamlet uses of Claudius and his workings; it is the word Claudius himself uses to describe his sin:

> O, my offence is rank, it smells to heaven.
>
> (III.iii.36)

"The Theme" by Bertram Joseph. From Conscience and the King *(London: Chatto & Windus, Ltd., 1953), pp. 130-151. This chapter has been extensively revised by the author for this edition, and is reprinted by his permission.*

In fighting his uncle, Hamlet is doing more than seeking personal revenge; he is fighting a source of evil, a rankness, a focus of corruption which will infect all Denmark and destroy it spiritually. Claudius gains his way by poisoning, literally and metaphorically, through the ear. The elder Hamlet has been killed by poison in "the porches of my ears" while asleep (like the King of the Dumbshow and *The Murder of Gonzago*); the whole country has been deceived by Claudius' words:

> the whole ear of Denmark
> Is by a forged process . . .
> Rankly abus'd.
>
> (I.v.36-8)

From very early in the play an important element of Hamlet's frustration is his inability to speak out. "But break my heart, for I must hold my tongue," ends his first soliloquy (I.ii.159); later he reproaches himself because he "can say nothing" about a real murder when the First Player says so much for Hecuba. But once he is sure of Claudius' guilt and the Ghost's honesty, Hamlet himself decides to attack through the ear in counteraction. He will "speak daggers" to his mother to win back her soul. Their edge makes Gertrude cry: "These words like daggers enter in my ears" (III.iv.95). When she has at last been brought to see Claudius as he is, she admits for the first time how vain has been her hope that Hamlet would accept him as a substitute for a real father, that her heart could shelter an undivided love for both the Prince and his "uncle-father":

> O, Hamlet, thou hast cleft my heart in twain.
>
> (III.iv.156)

He answers, "O, throw away the worser part of it," hoping that he has succeeded in excising the infection, her love for Claudius, by making her see that what Claudius is makes it impossible for her to love them both as she once loved son and husband.

To undo some of the harm done by Claudius, Hamlet has had to cut his mother with words. He does not totally regret this; it has been necessary and effective. But Polonius' death has not been necessary and makes the fight against Claudius more difficult. It is the first example of the price that will have to be paid before Claudius is destroyed. Repenting Polonius' death, Hamlet tells Gertrude: "I must be cruel only to be kind" (III.iv.178). After meeting the Ghost, as he went in with Marcellus and Horatio, Hamlet realized that this sort of thing was going to be unavoidable:

> The time is out of joint. O cursed spite,
> That ever I was born to set it right.
>
> (I.v.189-90)

Then he realized that he would have to "set" (in modern terminology, *reduce*) the dislocation. The Elizabethans regarded dislocation as a form of fracture, and therefore spoke of "setting" a limb that is out of joint, as we speak of setting one that is fractured. To put "the time" back in position would entail violence and pain, he recognized at that moment; he knew then he would have to be "cruel in order to be kind."

As we consider Hamlet's function of hurting to heal, the theme of the play begins to reveal itself. He must not only cut Claudius out of Gertrude's heart; he must excise the king, "this canker of our nature" (this corroding disease of our human body and mind) out of Denmark. He repeatedly speaks of himself as a physician or surgeon in relation to Claudius and his evil-doing. To know the truth Hamlet will tent (pierce) "to the quick," probing into the diseased ulcer of Claudius' conscience, until, metaphorically, the sound flesh winces.

Once he has seen Claudius "blench," Hamlet continues to think of himself as hurting to heal. When Guildenstern remonstrates that the king is "distemper'd" (a word with the sense of *ill* as well as *angry*) with choler (which means *fire* as well as *anger*), Hamlet says this is a matter for the royal doctor:

> . . . for me to put him to his purgation would perhaps plunge him into far more choler.

> (III.ii.298-300)

A few minutes later, when he spares the apparently praying Claudius, Hamlet repeats this threat in different words:

> Then trip him, that his heels may kick at heaven,
> And that his soul may be as damn'd and black
> As hell whereto it goes.

And the medical metaphor returns:

> This physic but prolongs thy sickly days.

> (III.iii.93-6)

Hamlet intends no cure for Claudius, who is to be destroyed, partly for vengeance, partly to save Denmark from corruption.

Although Hamlet has long realized he must be cruel to be kind, only with the killing of Polonius is he shocked into seeing clearly that his certainty about Claudius' guilt and the Ghost's honesty will give him no greater control of events.

> For this same lord
> I do repent; but Heaven hath pleas'd it so
> To punish me with this, and this with me,
> That I must be their scourge and minister.

> (III.iv.172-5)

He is beginning to grasp that he is being used as a servant of Heaven in some way that he does not understand, and this uncertainty still grieves him.

It takes the journey from Denmark, with the sudden, unexpected return, to open Hamlet's eyes fully. The success of his rashness has convinced him:

> There's a divinity that shapes our ends,
> Rough-hew them how we will.
>
> (V.ii.10-11)

Now he declares, "Why, even in that was heaven ordinant" when Horatio asks how the new commission was sealed (V.ii.48). How completely Hamlet is convinced that he must trust this divinity is revealed when he refuses to let Horatio change the arrangements for the apparently harmless duel of honor. Hamlet sees no point in trying to anticipate the future; he will trust to the inscrutable ways of providence. His original sense of being bound in duty to "set" the time "right," and his later urge to kill Claudius in revenge, have been transmuted into an assurance that whoever is to live or die, providence will be in control; he has come to see all his actions and those of everybody else in the play as serving the ends of providence.

It has escaped those critics who label Horatio a sceptic that he shares Hamlet's trust in providence. "Heaven will direct it," is his unperturbed reply when Marcellus asserts, "Something is rotten in the state of Denmark" (I.iv.91-2). And Hamlet's reference to the divinity "that shapes our ends" brings from Horatio complete agreement: "That is most certain" (V.ii.11).

Hamlet lives long enough to know that his trust in providence, even if it has meant his own death, has brought his revenge on Claudius in circumstances which will let Horatio tell all Denmark the truth. Hamlet no longer has to speak out and "appall the free"; for him "the rest is silence." He has destroyed Claudius, the source of infection, leaving it to another voice to:

> speak to th' yet unknowing world
> How these things came about. So shall you hear
> Of carnal, bloody and unnatural acts;
> Of accidental judgments, casual slaughters;
> Of deaths put on by cunning and forc'd cause;
> And, in this upshot, purposes mistook
> Fall'n on th' inventors' heads.
>
> (V.ii.371-7)

When Hamlet looks back on events up to the acceptance of the duel he finds no conflict between the part played by chance and that which he ascribes to providence. This is true of Horatio, too; he has much to contemplate when he comes to speak to the world. Hamlet's refusal to postpone the duel has had consequences: four deaths and the unmistakable exposure of Claudius for what he is, hypocrite, murderer, ingenious plotter. By the end of the play it is clear that by chance the players have come to Elsinore enabling Hamlet to use them; by chance Hamlet comes upon Claudius trying to pray; by chance Polonius, not Claudius, is killed. Chance brings the pirate ship; chance makes Gertrude unexpectedly drink the poison—her death being the first public exposure of Claudius as a murderer.

Horatio, who will tell all, knows that Heaven has directed chance; he trusts in providence. In the play he shares with Hamlet a belief held by Shakespeare's contemporaries. In real life Lancelot Andrewes declared in 1603 that the plague "is a thing causal not casual; it comes not merely by chance, but hath somewhat, some cause that procureth it." That cause he found in providence:

> Sure if a sparrow fall not to the ground without the providence of God, of which two are sold for a farthing; much less doth any man, or woman, which are more worth than many sparrows.[1]

Andrewes is sure that no man comes "to his end (as we call it) by casualty," but that God "delivers him so to die." *Casualty* is Andrewes' word for *chance;* he thinks of it as Horatio thinks of *casual slaughters.* For him in real life, as for Hamlet and Horatio in the play, chance or Fortune is the instrument of providence. The same doctrine occurs in the familiar *Sermon for Rogation Week* (an official Homily):

> The paynims' philosophers and poets did err, which took Fortune, and made her a goddess, to be honoured for such things . . . Epicures they be that imagine he (God) walketh about the coasts of the heavens, and hath no respect of these inferior things, but that all these things should proceed either by chance or at adventure, or else by disposition of fortune, and God to have no stroke in them.[2]

The unlearned reader was thus instructed "Of Fortune" in Baldwin's popular *Moral Philosophy:*

> This term of Fortune or chance, used of men, proceeded first out of ignorance and want to true knowledge, not considering what God is, and by whose only fore-sight and providence, all things in the world are seen of him before they come to pass.[3]

---

[1] *XCVI Sermons* (1629), p. 160.
[2] *Certain Sermons or Homilies* (1623), II, 223.
[3] (?1640), Folio 157 r⁰.

From Boethius the Renaissance inherited the view of Fortune, not as blind necessity, but as the instrument of providence, interacting with the characters of men to achieve divine purposes. This is no determinist view of life. The end is planned, but the manner in which it is attained depends upon the reactions of individual human beings to situations created by fortune. Boethius ends his dialogue on the part played by fortune in human affairs with the demonstration by Philosophy that human will is free:

> And so the freedom of men's will remains inviolate, and the laws are not unjust which assign rewards and punishments for wills unbound by any necessity. Moreover, God who has knowledge of all things remains looking down from on high, and the ever-present eternity of His vision agrees with the future character of our acts, dispensing to the good rewards, to the evil punishment.[4]

The influence of *The Consolations of Philosophy* was virtually inescapable in Shakespeare's lifetime. Two of the many translations are noteworthy: that of Queen Elizabeth in 1593, and the version by one "I. T." in 1609 which is still the basis of the standard Loeb edition. There is no need to be surprised at finding "Boethian" thinking in an official Homily, in a popular work on Philosophy, in Milton (who speaks of "that power/Which erring men call Chance")[5] or in *Hamlet*. It is because the Prince is thinking in this way that he can perceive the working of providence in his own rash actions.

> Rashly,
> And prais'd be rashness for it—let us know,
> Our indiscretion sometime serves us well,
> When our deep plots do pall; and that should learn us
> There's a divinity that shapes our ends,
> Rough-hew them how we will.
>
>   (V.ii.6-11)

As Hamlet delivers this comment we find our subconscious reactions to the ironies and reversals of the plot becoming crystallized in a consciousness that the death of Claudius has been delayed for other more fundamental reasons than Hamlet's or Claudius' own feelings of expediency. By stealing a kingdom and a brother's life Claudius led Fortinbras to see an opportunity for regaining lost territory from a state apparently "disjoint and out of frame." As a result extra guards were posted; they saw the Ghost. They asked Horatio to watch with them (he was in Denmark for the dead king's funeral), with the

---

[4] *The Consolations of Philosophy with English Translation*, rev. H. F. Stewart (1918), p. 411.

[5] *Comus, A Masque* (1634), ll. 586-7.

result that at his suggestion Hamlet, not Claudius, was told of the apparition. But Hamlet, not trusting the Ghost, waits for proof. When he has proof he waits again, in order to deny Claudius "hire and salary." Nevertheless a divinity has shaped the ends, so that Hamlet's rough-hewing (such as the mistake with Polonius) contributes to a chain of events involving the journey and return, leading through the duel to the moment when Claudius is killed and his guilt can be exposed.

When Sir Thomas Browne contemplated his experience of such changes and reversals in real life, he declared that while God has shown the "ordinary and open way of his providence" in Nature ("the art of God"), there is another way "full of meanders and labyrinths." This "more particular and obscure method of his providence" concerns itself with individuals and is called fortune, "that serpentine and crooked line, whereby he draws those actions his wisdom intends, in a more unknown and secret way." Browne is sure that in every man's life, as in his own, there are "certain rubs, doublings and wrenches, which pass a while under the effects of chance, but at the last, well examined, prove the mere hand of God." [6]

Horatio and Hamlet recognize the hand of God alone (*the mere hand of God*) beneath the "rubs, doublings and wrenches" in that "serpentine and crooked line" which runs from the oath on the battlements to the duel with Laertes. Hamlet's defiance of "augury" is a refusal to try to probe the "more unknown and secret way" of God's providence. Whatever happens in life, however important or unimportant, is part of that secret way.

When Hamlet declares with assurance, "There is a special providence in the fall of a sparrow," his thinking agrees with that of Perkins, the influential Cambridge divine, who writes of Special Providence as the way in which God "ordereth all things and directeth them to good ends." It involves "the very least thing that is in heaven or earth, as to the *sparrows,* and to oxen, and *the hair of our heads.*" [7]

According to this doctrine our ends are shaped by a divinity aware of everything that will happen throughout time, down to the slightest detail, who is yet content in His omnipotence to work through human beings endowed with free will, as well as through the separate incidents popularly regarded as chance. Hamlet echoes and is echoed by innumerable preachers, who celebrated the preservation of England from the Armada and the Gunpowder Plot, and that of James I from the Conspiracy of the Gowries while still in his native Scotland. "The very *minims* of the world, His mercy leaves them not destitute," exults Lancelot Andrewes in his seventh annual sermon on the Gun-

[6] *Religio Medici* (written in 1635), in *Works,* ed. G. Keynes (1928), Vol. 1, p. 23.
[7] W. Perkins, *An Exposition of the Creed* (1595), in *Works* (1616), Vol. 1, p. 155.

powder Plot. This mercy extends to "the sparrow of half a farthing"; God will not let even a sparrow "light on the ground without His providence." [8] Providence is served by any human action, whatever its motive. Particular cause for delight was found in the fact that "the Emperor Octavius served God's purpose, yet knew nothing of him" (the words are Latimer's), when the edict went out for every man in the Roman Empire to return to his birthplace; thus Jesus was born in Bethlehem.[9]

Hamlet is sure that he, too, will serve God's purpose; whether he lives or dies now, whether he kills Claudius or not, is a matter for providence to decide. In real life Latimer shared the belief which we find in Hamlet in the play:

> For every man hath a certain time appointed him of God, and God hideth that same time from us. For some die in young age, some in old age, according as it pleaseth him. . . . But of that we may be sure, there shall not fall one hair from our head without his will; and we shall not die before our time that God hath appointed unto us.

Just as Hamlet is sure "the readiness is all," so Latimer declares God "hath not manifested to us the time, because he would have us at all times ready." [10] With "the readiness is all," however, Hamlet speaks not only of his own preparedness for death, but of his function in a larger plan. He believes that his death and that of Claudius will come only if the moment is ripe. Revenge will come and Denmark will be purged of corruption only at the right moment for providence. Without the approval of providence, no human planning will overcome the king. Again we find one of Shakespeare's contemporaries in agreement with this point of view, remarking in *The French Academy:*

> . . . among those fruits which attain to maturity and ripeness, all have not one and the self time of ripening, but every one hath his proper season: and those that are most forward and soonest ripe, are of the shortest continuance; and quickly gone. This self same thing also we see to be observed in the life of men, and in the course of this world.[11]

Hamlet's answer to Horatio refers both to "the life of men" and "the course of this world." Most appropriately, in what seems to be the speech which Hamlet has written into *The Murder of Gonzago,* the Player King complains:

> Purpose is but the slave to memory,
> Of violent birth, but poor validity;

8 *Works* (1854), Vol. 4, p. 328.
9 *Works,* ed. Corrie (1845), p. 97.
10 *Sixth Sermon on the Lord's Prayer,* in *Ibid.,* p. 416.
11 P. de la Primaudaye, *The French Academy, Part Two* (1594), p. 421.

> Which now, the fruit unripe, sticks on the tree;
> But fall unshaken when they mellow be.

(III.ii.183-6)

We find the same thinking in an Elizabethan letter of consolation to the mother of two young noblemen recently dead:

> Among fruit we see some apples are soon ripe, and fall from the tree in the midst of summer, other be still green and tarry till winter, and hereupon are commonly called winter fruit.[12]

When Hamlet agonized over his failure as he watched the army of Fortinbras, he did not yet realize that he was shaking a tree whose fruit were unripe. But when he defies augury he knows that the fruit "will fall unshaken when they mellow be." No man, he asserts, can be expected to know beforehand when that moment will come. Indeed, no man can expect to know so much about any undertaking on which he is engaged as to be sure that he has brought it to a satisfactory state of development, that he can leave it, confident that it will succeed.

Hamlet actually says this explicitly in the Good Quarto (1604):

> . . . since no man of ought he leaves, knowes what ist to leave betimes.

The sense is clear if we read "of ought he leaves" in parenthesis— "since no man, of ought he leaves, knowes, . . ." etc. Then the whole statement can be glossed:

> . . . since no man knows enough about anything he leaves to know that he leaves it betimes.

Betimes refers both to the time of leaving and the state of the business which is left.

Hamlet, just before his death, and Horatio, immediately after it, are both confident that beneath the labyrinthine course of events in Denmark lies "the mere hand of God." That is why, refusing to change arrangements, the Prince ends, "Let be," meaning both "leave it alone" and "let it happen." With Hamlet dead, Horatio has more than a blind faith in providence. Now he can perceive what has been happening; he can call attention not only to "accidental judgments"; he can explain them, how they came about "in this upshot."

The events of the plot make sense of, and are made sense by, Hamlet's and Horatio's references to providence. It is not enough to kill Claudius; the king must also be unmistakably exposed for what he is. In the whole play there is only one moment when this can happen; and when it happens it is a culmination of a long serpentine course

---

12 T. Wilson, *The Art of Rhetoric* (1560), repr. Mair (1909), pp. 83f.

of events linking Hamlet's doubts, his antic disposition, sparing of
Claudius at one moment, killing of Polonius, his journey from and
back to Denmark, with Claudius' treachery with sword and drink.

In the end Claudius' death and exposure come from his own plot-
ting, not Hamlet's. The Prince has relinquished his horrifying intention of killing Claudius about some deed "which hath no relish of
salvation in it." Claudius is killed about some such business, but it is
the result of his own contrivance. Hamlet has given up planning. He
does not choose a foil with intent to kill Claudius, but with the
generous determination to be reconciled to Laertes. Claudius' death
is due to his own "purposes mistook"; he is a perfect illustration of
Gertrude's *sententia:*

> So full of artless jealousy is guilt,
> It spills itself in fearing to be spilt.
> (IV.v.19-20)

Gertrude's words express her own guilty fears. They are in couplet,
however, in accordance with Renaissance classical teaching, to direct
our attention to their validity as a comment on the action of the play.
"So full of artless anxiety not to be caught unawares is guilt, that it
destroys and exposes itself in its fear of destruction and exposure."
Claudius has really arranged his own "accidental judgment" in trying
to evade it.

When Andrewes spoke of similar examples of the workings of
providence in the Biblical story of Esther, he rejoiced that God cir-
cumvented Haman's cunning, diverting "the current in a quite contrary way, clean back upon Haman, to overflow him and to drown
him" instead of his quarry, Mordecai.[13] "Very oft doth God betray
bad enterprises by such (one would think them) mere casual events." [14]
The play *Hamlet* prompts the same comment. The overt statements
from Horatio and Hamlet, the sententia from Gertrude, the events of
the plot, the ultimate death and exposure of Claudius, all justify a
comment such as Hall's on the obscure course of divine justice: "He
knows how, by one man's sin to punish the sin of another, and by
both their sin and punishments to glorify himself," using their evil
"to his own holy purposes." [15] In real life England, as in imaginary
Denmark, evil can fail when almost triumphant. Browne loved to
recall the chance events by which providence saved his country from
the Armada and the Gunpowder Plot.[16] So did Andrewes:

---

13 *Works* (1854), Vol. 4, pp. 400f.
14 *Ibid.,* pp. 141f.
15 Hall, *Works* (1837), Vol. 1, pp. 360 and 155.
16 *Religio Medici,* in *Works,* Vol. 1, pp. 23f.

. . . and all the goodly *cobweb,* that was so many months in spinning and weaving, comes me a *broom,* and in a minute snaps it down and destroys it quite.[17]

Hamlet is a triumphant assertion of what its author sees as a consolation in life's uncertainties. The Prince is a servant of providence; he must be cruel like a surgeon in order to be kind; he cannot achieve his revenge until the time is ripe, and that has been foreseen by the divinity "that shapes our ends." The moment, when it comes, emerges from Claudius' own planning, not from the efforts of Hamlet. The more we contemplate the events of the play, the more they make us aware of the "mere hand" of providence destroying evil.

[17] *Works,* Vol. 4, p. 314.

PART TWO

View Points

E. E. Stoll: Hamlet's Fault in the Light of Other Tragedies

It now seems probable that a reproach may, in effect, be no more than an exhortation; and of this sort in the main are the Ghost's and Hamlet's own:

> Do you not come your tardy son to chide
> That, lapst in time and passion, lets go by
> The important acting of your dread command?

> *Ghost.* Do not forget, this visitation
> Is but to whet thy almost blunted purpose.

That may be, not a judgment on Hamlet's character, but a reflection on his conduct in this particular matter, with a practical end in view. The Ghost at least is not nearly so hard on the young Prince as are Belimperia and Isabella on Hieronimo.[1] In any case, the Ghost and Hamlet too take it for granted that the youth is equal to the task. The Ghost reproaches Hamlet; Hamlet chides himself: but no doubt of his powers or intentions is ever expressed by either.

So it is in Seneca. Mere exhortation, not damaging revelation of character, is the function of self-reproaches in the old Latin dramatist, artistic sponsor of Kyd and Marston, and creator of the revenge-play type. In the *Thyestes* Atreus broods over his remissness somewhat like Hieronimo and Hamlet.

> O Soul so sluggish, spiritless, and weak,

he cries; but like them, it would seem, he is not ordinarily sluggish and not spiritless or weak at all. And the same, of course, may be said of those far from weak or spiritless ladies, Medea and Clytemnestra, who chide and scold themselves only to spur themselves on.

> Why, sluggish soul, dost thou safe counsel seek?
> Why hesitate?

From Hamlet: An Historical and Comparative Study *(Minneapolis, University of Minnesota Press, 1919). Reprinted by permission of the publisher. This selection is from sections 2 and 7 of Chapter II.*
[1] In *The Spanish Tragedy* by Thomas Kyd—ED.

cries the latter. In these cases, to be sure, there is no such long interval of delay as in *Hamlet;* but delay of some sort there is in all classical and Renaissance revenge tragedies, and these exhortations serve to motive it. They motive it, that is, not in the psychological sense of grounding it in character, but of explaining it and bridging it over. They motive it by reminding the audience that the main business in hand, though retarded, is not lost to view. They motive it by showing the audience that the hero, even in his delay, is a conscious and responsible and (so far) consistent being. In short, they give a reason for the delay, not the "good" and fundamental reason demanded by the author of *Some Remarks,* but a better reason than none. They provide an epical motive, if I may so call it, rather than a dramatic one.

*   *   *

The technique, then, the similarity of the technique to that in other Shakespearean and Elizabethan plays and to what we can learn of that in the old play, the unanimous testimony of the two centuries nearest the poet,—all these things conspire together to prove that Hamlet was meant to be an ideal character. He has no tragic fault, any more than has Romeo—like Romeo's his fault is not in himself but in his stars. And thus conceived, he seems much more Shakespearean and Elizabethan—being less Coleridgean and German. As conceived by the Romanticists he is an anomaly—unlike any other character of the time.

J. Dover Wilson: Antic Disposition

[See *Hamlet,* II.ii.159–185 in which Polonius proposes to use his daughter Ophelia as a bait for Hamlet, while Polonius and Claudius conceal themselves behind an arras; at which point Hamlet enters unexpectedly and is spoken to by Polonius—Ed.]

Everything that Hamlet here says is capable of an equivocal interpretation reflecting upon Polonius and Ophelia. "Fishmonger," as many commentators have noted, means a pander or procurer; "carrion" was a common expression at that time for "flesh" in the carnal sense; while the quibble in "conception" needs no explaining. And when I asked myself why Hamlet should suddenly call Polonius a bawd and his daughter a prostitute—for that is what it all amounts to—I could discover but one possible answer to my question, namely that "Fishmonger" and the rest follows immediately upon "loose

From What Happens in Hamlet *(New York: Cambridge University Press, 1959), pp. 105-108. Copyright © 1959 by Cambridge University Press. Reprinted by permission of the author and the publisher. This study first appeared in 1935.*

my daughter to him." Nor was this the end of the matter. For what
might Hamlet mean by his sarcastic advice to the father not to let
the daughter "walke i'th Sunne," or by the reference to the sun
breeding in the "carrion" exposed to it? Bearing in mind Hamlet's
punning retort "I am too much in the 'son,' " in answer to Claudius's
unctuous question at I.ii.64,

> And now my cousin Hamlet, and my son,
> How is it that the clouds still hang on you?—

and recalling Falstaff's apostrophe to Prince Hal: "Shall the blessed
sun of heaven prove a micher and eat blackberries? a question not
to be asked. Shall the son of England prove a thief and take purses?
a question to be asked," is it not obvious that Hamlet here means
by "Sunne" the sun or son of Denmark, the heir apparent, in other
words himself? And if so, "let her not walke i'th Sunne" is to be
paraphrased "take care that you do not loose your daughter to me!"
    What then? *Hamlet must have overheard what Polonius said to
the King.* The context allows no escape from this conclusion, inas-
much as what Hamlet says to Polonius is only intelligible if the
conclusion be allowed. It remains to examine the text in order to
discover, if possible, what Shakespeare's intentions, clearly impaired
in some way by corruption, may have been. We are left, of course, to
conjecture, but even so we are not entirely without clues. Says
Polonius:

> You know sometimes he walks four hours together
> Here in the lobby;

and as he speaks we may imagine him jerking a thumb over his
shoulder towards the inner stage before which the three plotters
stand, their faces to the audience. Words and the action are a direct
invitation to the spectators to look in that direction; and, as they
do so, Hamlet enters the inner stage from the door at the back,
his eyes upon his book, quite unconscious at first that his uncle, his
mother, and Polonius are on the outer stage, which stands for the
audience chamber of the castle. In short, "Here in the lobby" is
equivalent to a stage direction, and marks with practical certainty the
moment at which Hamlet comes in and the place of his entry. And
it is the right moment; for the entry should seem unquestionably
accidental, lest the audience should suspect him of deliberate spying.
It would never do, for example, to let him linger in his place of
concealment. Between the King's question "How may me try it
further?" and his resolve "We will try it" there lie eight lines of
dialogue. They just give Hamlet time to enter the lobby, grow

conscious of voices in the larger chamber beyond, pause for a moment beside the entrance thereto, compose his features, and come forward. But brief as the period is, it is long enough for him to take in the whole eavesdropping plot and to implicate Ophelia beyond possibility of doubt in his ears as one of his uncle's minions.

*   *   *

Hamlet's accidental discovery of the intention to spy upon him has a bearing much wider than his attitude towards Ophelia. Indeed, the manner in which it eases the general working of the plot is strong testimony in its favor. As we shall find, it constitutes the mainspring of the events that follow in acts II and III; it renders the nunnery scene playable and intelligible as never before; it adds all kinds of fresh light and shade to the play scene. In a word, its recovery means the restoration of a highly important piece of the dramatic structure. For the moment, however, let us confine our attention to the matter in hand; and see what it tells us about Hamlet's relations with the daughter of Polonius. Here its value is at once obvious, since it casts its light backward as well as forward and enables us for the first time to see these relations in proper perspective and as a connected whole.

Ernest Jones: Hamlet and Oedipus

That Hamlet is suffering from an internal conflict the essential nature of which is inaccessible to his introspection is evidenced by the following considerations. Throughout the play we have the clearest picture of a man who sees his duty plain before him, but who shirks it at every opportunity and suffers in consequence the most intense remorse. To paraphrase Sir James Paget's well-known description of hysterical paralysis: Hamlet's advocates say he cannot do his duty, his detractors say he will not, whereas the truth is that he cannot will. Further than this, the deficient will-power is localized to the one question of killing his uncle; it is what may be termed a *specific abulia*. Now instances of such specific abulias in real life invariably prove, when analyzed, to be due to an unconscious repulsion against the act that cannot be performed (or else against something closely associated with the act, so that the idea of the act

From Hamlet and Oedipus *(London: Victor Gollancz, Ltd., 1949; New York: W. W. Norton & Company, Inc., 1949), pp. 52-53, 59-60, and 82. Copyright © 1949 by Ernest Jones. Reprinted by permission of the publishers. This study appeared in its original form in 1910.*

becomes also involved in the repulsion). In other words, whenever a person cannot bring himself to do something that every conscious consideration tells him he should do—and which he may have the strongest conscious desire to do—it is always because there is some hidden reason why a part of him doesn't want to do it; this reason he will not own to himself and is only dimly if at all aware of. That is exactly the case with Hamlet.

*   *   *

It only remains to add the obvious corollary that, as the herd unquestionably selects from the "natural" instincts the sexual one on which to lay its heaviest ban, so it is the various psycho-sexual trends that are most often "repressed" by the individual. We have here the explanation of the clinical experience that the more intense and the more obscure is a given case of deep mental conflict the more certainly will it be found on adequate analysis to center about a sexual problem. On the surface, of course, this does not appear so, for, by means of various psychological defensive mechanisms, the depression, doubt, despair, and other manifestations of the conflict are transferred on to more tolerable and permissible topics, such as anxiety about worldly success or failure, about immortality and the salvation of the soul, philosophical considerations about the value of life, the future of the world, and so on.

Bearing these considerations in mind, let us return to Hamlet.

*   *   *

Now comes the father's death and the mother's second marriage. The association of the idea of sexuality with his mother, buried since infancy, can no longer be concealed from his consciousness. As Bradley well says: "Her son was forced to see in her action not only an astounding shallowness of feeling, but an eruption of coarse sensuality, 'rank and gross,' speeding posthaste to its horrible delight." Feelings which once, in the infancy of long ago, were pleasurable desires can now, because of his repressions, only fill him with repulsion. The long "repressed" desire to take his father's place in his mother's affection is stimulated to unconscious activity by the sight of someone usurping this place exactly as he himself had once longed to do. More, this someone was a member of the same family, so that the actual usurpation further resembled the imaginary one in being incestuous. Without his being in the least aware of it these ancient desires are ringing in his mind, are once more struggling to find conscious expression, and need such an expenditure of energy in to "repress" them that he is reduced to the deplorable mental he himself so vividly depicts.

C. S. Lewis: Hamlet—The Prince or the Poem?

For what, after all, is happening to us when we read any of Hamlet's great speeches? We see visions of the flesh dissolving into a dew, of the world like an unweeded garden. We think of memory reeling in its "distracted globe." We watch him scampering hither and thither like a maniac to avoid the voices wherewith he is haunted. Someone says "Walk out of the air," and we hear the words "Into my grave" spontaneously respond to it. We think of being bounded in a nut-shell and king of infinite space: but for bad dreams. There's the trouble, for "I am most dreadfully attended." We see the picture of a dull and muddy-mettled rascal, a John-a-dreams, somehow unable to move while ultimate dishonor is done him. We listen to his fear lest the whole thing may be an illusion due to melancholy. We get the sense of sweet relief at the words "shuffled off this mortal coil" but mixed with the bottomless doubt about what may follow then. We think of bones and skulls, of women breeding sinners, and of how some, to whom all this experience is a sealed book, can yet dare death and danger "for an eggshell." But do we really enjoy these things, do we go back to them, because they show us Hamlet's character? Are they, from *that* point of view, so very interesting? Does the mere fact that a young man, literally haunted, dispossessed, and lacking friends, should feel thus, tell us anything remarkable? Let me put my question in another way. If instead of the speeches he actually utters about the firmament and man in his scene with Rosencrantz and Guildenstern Hamlet had merely said, "I don't seem to enjoy things the way I used to," and talked in that fashion throughout, should we find him interesting? I think the answer is "Not very." It may be replied that if he talked commonplace prose he would reveal his character less vividly. I am not so sure. He would certainly have revealed *something* less vividly; but would that something be himself? It seems to me that "this majestical roof" and "What a piece of work is a man" give me primarily an impression not of the sort of person he must be to lose the estimation of things but of the things themselves and their great value; and that I should be able to discern, though with very faint interest, the same condition of loss in a personage who was quite unable so to put before me what he was losing. And I do not think it true to reply that he would be a different character if he spoke less poetically. This point is often misunderstood.

From Proceedings of the British Academy, *XXXVIII (London: Oxford University Press, 1942), 14-15. Copyright 1942 by Oxford University Press. Reprinted by permission of the publisher. This selection is a brief excerpt from the lecture.*

We sometimes speak as if the characters in whose mouths Shakespeare puts great poetry were poets: in the sense that Shakespeare was depicting men of poetical genius. But surely this is like thinking that Wagner's Wotan is the dramatic portrait of a baritone? In opera song is the medium by which the representation is made and not part of the thing represented. The actors sing; the dramatic personages are feigned to be speaking. The only character who sings dramatically in *Figaro* is Cherubino. Similarly in poetical drama poetry is the medium, not part of the delineated characters. While the actors speak poetry written for them by the poet, the dramatic personages are supposed to be merely talking. If ever there is occasion to *represent* poetry (as in the play scene from *Hamlet*), it is put into a different metre and strongly stylized so as to prevent confusion.

I trust that my conception is now becoming clear. I believe that we read Hamlet's speeches with interest chiefly because they describe so well a certain spiritual region through which most of us have passed and anyone in his circumstances might be expected to pass, rather than because of our concern to understand how and why this particular man entered it.

G. *Wilson Knight:* The Embassy of Death

Hamlet is inhuman. He has seen through humanity. And this inhuman cynicism, however justifiable in this case, on the plane of causality and individual responsibility, is a deadly and venomous thing. Instinctively the creatures of earth—Laertes, Polonius, Ophelia, Rosencrantz and Guildenstern, league themselves with Claudius: they are of his kind. They sever themselves from Hamlet. Laertes sternly warns Ophelia against her intimacy with Hamlet, so does Polonius. They are, in fact, all leagued against him, they are puzzled by him or fear him: he has no friend except Horatio, and Horatio, after the ghost scenes, becomes a queer shadowy character who rarely gets beyond "E'en so, my lord," "My lord—," and such-like phrases. The other persons are firmly drawn, in the round, creatures of flesh and blood. But Hamlet is not of flesh and blood, he is a spirit of penetrating intellect and cynicism and misery, without faith in himself or anyone else, murdering his love of Ophelia, on the brink of insanity, taking delight in cruelty, torturing Claudius, wringing his mother's heart, a poison in the midst of the healthy bustle of the court. He is a superman among men. And he is a superman because he has

From "The Embassy of Death," in The Wheel of Fire *(London: Methuen & Co., Ltd., 1930, rev. ed. 1954), pp. 38-39. Copyright © 1954 by Methuen & Co., Ltd. Reprinted by permission of the publisher.*

walked and held converse with Death, and his consciousness works in terms of Death and the Negation of Cynicism. He has seen the truth, not alone of Denmark, but of humanity, of the universe: and the truth is evil. Thus Hamlet is an element of evil in the state of Denmark. The poison of his mental existence spreads outwards among things of flesh and blood, like acid eating into metal. They are helpless before his very inactivity and fall one after the other, like victims of an infectious disease. They are strong with the strength of health —but the demon of Hamlet's mind is a stronger thing than they. Futilely they try to get him out of their country; anything to get rid of him, he is not safe. But he goes with a cynical smile, and is no sooner gone than he is back again in their midst, meditating in graveyards, at home with Death. Not till it has slain all, is the demon that grips Hamlet satisfied. And last it slays Hamlet himself:

> The spirit that I have seen
> May be the devil . . .
>
> (II.ii.627)

It was.

It was the devil of the knowledge of death, which possesses Hamlet and drives him from misery and pain to increasing bitterness, cynicism, murder, and madness. He has indeed bought converse with his father's spirit at the price of enduring and spreading hell on Earth. But however much we may sympathize with Ophelia, with Polonius, Rosencrantz, Guildenstern, the Queen, and Claudius, there is one reservation to be made. It is Hamlet who is right. What he says and thinks of them is true, and there is no fault in his logic. His own mother is indeed faithless, and the prettiness of Ophelia does in truth enclose a spirit as fragile and untrustworthy as her earthly beauty; Polonius is "a foolish prating knave"; Rosencrantz and Guildenstern are time-servers and flatterers; Claudius, whose benevolence hides the guilt of murder, is, by virtue of that fact, "a damned smiling villain." In the same way the demon of cynicism which is in the mind of the poet and expresses itself in the figures of this play, has always this characteristic: it is right. One cannot argue with the cynic. It is unwise to offer him battle. For in the warfare of logic it will be found that he has all the guns.

Salvador de Madariaga: Rosencrantz and Guildenstern

This procrastination cannot be due to an instinctive and fastidious repugnance to killing, for Hamlet kills Polonius, and Laertes, and

From On Hamlet, *2nd ed. (London: Frank Cass & Co., Ltd., 1964), pp. 14-16. Copyright 1948 by Salvador de Madariaga. Reprinted by permission of the author and the publisher. This study first appeared in 1948.*

in the end the King himself; and he dispatches Rosencrantz and Guildenstern to their doom with true alacrity. Whence then does it come?

The answer will be found by examining all these cases. And before them all, let us look at those two lines in I.4.

> unhand me gentlemen,
> By heaven I'll make a ghost of him that lets me!

It is one of the key points in the drawing of his character. When it comes to doing what he is determined to do, he will not hesitate to kill even his closest friend, for Horatio is one of the gentlemen whom he threatens sword in hand. Hamlet's spontaneous tendencies are therefore essentially individualistic; and, the point must be emphasized, not even death of others, if need be, will stand in his way.

This is the Hamlet whose behavior towards Rosencrantz and Guildenstern we are now to study. They were his friends, and we know from his mother that he had much talked of them and that

> two men there are not living
> To whom he more adheres.

The two young men receive from the King a commission which, whatever the King's secret intentions may be, is honorable. Hamlet, the King in fact tells them, is not what he was. The cause of the change "I cannot dream of." Therefore, I beg you

> so by your companies
> To draw him on to pleasures, and to gather
> So much as from occasion you may glean
> Whether aught to us unknown afflicts him thus
> That opened lies within our remedy.

Guildenstern's words show that the two young men understand their work in an irreproachable way:

> Heaven make our presence and our practices
> Pleasant and helpful to him.

They enter upon their new duties at a later stage in the same scene. Cordial and lighthearted, the meeting of the three young men leads to some fencing of wits on ambition; for Rosencrantz and Guildenstern, who know nothing about King Hamlet's murder, naturally assume that the trouble with Hamlet is frustrated ambition (and so in part it is): Hamlet, of course, parries, and as he tries to move off, his two companions, in strict obedience to their master, the King, say: "We'll wait upon you." This raises his suspicions. "But, in the

beaten way of friendship, what make you at Elsinore?" They are put
out. Very likely they had not expected this alertness in a Hamlet
the King had depicted

> So much from th'understanding of himself.

They try to plot a concerted answer, but in the end are honest to
him; and to his direct question they return a direct answer: "My
lord, we were sent for."

This scene is typical. Bearing in mind that, for Rosencrantz and
Guildenstern, the King was their legitimate sovereign, and that for
all they knew, Hamlet was at least "queer," the two young men acquit
themselves of their delicate duties with skill and dignity. They do
make mistakes later, and, as Guildenstern openly avows: "O my lord,
if my duty be too bold, my love is too unmannerly." But this other
scene is one in which Hamlet's whole inconsidered egotism shows
itself unashamed. He is, of course, excited by the triumph of his
stratagem, the play, whereby he has proved the Ghost right and the
King a criminal; yet this circumstance merely raises the pitch of his
mood, without in any way altering the essence of his character. His
behavior towards Rosencrantz and Guildenstern is rude in the extreme. "This courtesy is not of the right breed," says Guildenstern;
and when Rosencrantz points out to him "you once did love me,"
his answer is: "And do still, by these pickers and stealers." He has a
case; of course he has a case. And he puts it with unforgettable beauty
and truth in his apologue on the recorder. " 'Sblood, do you think I
am easier to be played on than a pipe?" And one can conceive his
irritation at being followed and accompanied when he would prefer
to be alone. But, when all is said and pondered on his behalf, the
scene remains an exhibition of complete self-centeredness and of utter
disregard for the feelings of others.

Peter Alexander: The Complete Man

Tragedy, Shakespeare had come to see when he was writing *Hamlet,*
is a kind of consecration of the common elements of man's moral life.
Shakespeare introduces the common man in Hamlet not for what
we are apt to think of as his "commonness" but for this strange power
however you care to name it that he possesses—we have used *areté,*
or virtue, or we might have borrowed from Henry James "the individ-

From Hamlet, Father and Son *(Oxford: The Clarendon Press, 1955), pp. 183-185.
Copyright © 1955 by the Clarendon Press. Reprinted by permission of the author
and the publisher. This selection is the ending of the final chapter, "The Complete
Man."*

ual vision of decency." In Tragedy there is no longer a Chorus moving round the altar of a god; but if Proust is right the spectators are
still participants in a supernatural ceremony.

   Perhaps I may put the aspect of Tragedy I wish to keep before you
more clearly by drawing on Professor Harbage's study of Shakespeare's
ideal man. Collecting the approving references he finds that this ideal
man is soldierly, scholarly, and honest. If these men seem to lack the
larger idealism that is so common and abundant in our own generation, there is no suspicion that Shakespeare's men will fail to back
with their own skin their apparently modest programs. As Professor
Harbage says: "All soldierly, scholarly, honest men are potential martyrs"—you can substitute for "martyrs" tragic figures. Of that Shakespearean type Hamlet is the ideal. Shakespeare had before him in
Saxo and Belleforest what was presented as an ideal type. This type
Shakespeare transformed. To what may be called *the instinctive wisdom of antiquity and her heroic passions,* represented so impressively
by Hamlet's father, Shakespeare has united *the meditative wisdom of
later ages* in Hamlet himself. There is no surrender of the old pieties,
and the idea of the drama comes from the impact of new circumstances upon the old forms of feeling and estimation; there is a conflict between new exigencies and old pieties, that have somehow to
be reconciled. The play dramatizes the perpetual struggle to which all
civilization that is genuine is doomed. To live up to its own ideals it
has to place itself at a disadvantage with the cunning and treacherous.
The problem Mr. Chandler [1] sets his hero is infinitely complicated in
Hamlet—to be humane without loss of toughness. The hero must
touch both extremes: without one he is just brutal, lacking the other
he is merely wet. The problem Mr. Chandler has posed for the writer
of the story of crime Shakespeare solved, I am suggesting to you, just
after his thirty-fifth year, when he finally transformed the ancient
saga-like story preserved for us by Saxo into the play we know as
Hamlet.

   [1] Raymond Chandler, a modern writer of detective stories, who describes his fic-
tional hero in terms also applicable to Hamlet: a man who is typical of humanity
and yet unusual, a humane and honorable person with a disgust for sham who must
combat human meanness by sometimes ruthless means—ED.

Chronology of Important Dates

The dates of plays are approximate, and refer to first performances. They are based on Alfred Harbage, *Annals of English Drama, 975-1700,* revised by S. Schoenbaum (Philadelphia, 1964).

Shakespeare	*The Age*
1558	Accession of Queen Elizabeth I.
1564 Shakespeare born at Stratford-upon-Avon; baptized April 26.	
1576	James Burbage built the first permanent playhouse in England, named the Theater, in the suburbs north of London.
1582 Shakespeare married to Anne Hathaway (November).	
1583-85 Susanna born (May 26) followed by the twins, Hamnet and Judith (February 2).	
1587	*The Spanish Tragedy* by Thomas Kyd.
1588	The English Navy defeated the Spanish Armada. *Endymion* by John Lyly.
1591-92 The three *Henry VI* plays; *The Comedy of Errors*. The first reference in print to Shakespeare in London: Robert Greene's satirical comment on "Shake-scene."	
1592	*Doctor Faustus* and *Edward II* by Christopher Marlowe.

1593-94	*Venus and Adonis* and *The Rape of Lucrece* dedicated to the Earl of Southampton. *Titus Andronicus; The Taming of the Shrew; Richard III; Two Gentlemen of Verona.* Shakespeare joined in forming the Lord Chamberlain's company of actors.	
1595-96	*A Midsummer Night's Dream; Richard II; Romeo and Juliet; King John; The Merchant of Venice.* The death of Hamnet.	
1597-98	The two parts of *Henry IV; Much Ado about Nothing.* Shakespeare purchased New Place in Stratford. Shakespeare praised by Francis Meres as England's leading playwright.	
1599-1600	*As You Like It; Henry V; Julius Caesar; Twelfth Night; The Merry Wives of Windsor.* Shakespeare's company moved to the new Globe Theater.	*The Shoemakers' Holiday* (1599) by Thomas Dekker.
1601-1602	*Hamlet; All's Well that Ends Well; Troilus and Cressida.*	*The Poetaster* (1601) by Ben Jonson and the so-called "War of the Theaters." The abortive rebellion of the Earl of Essex.
1603-1604	*Measure for Measure; Othello.* Shakespeare's company became the King's Men.	(1603) The death of Elizabeth and the accession of James I.
1605-1606	*Macbeth; King Lear.*	*Volpone* by Ben Jonson (1606).
1607-1608	*Antony and Cleopatra; Timon of Athens; Coriolanus; Pericles.*	
1609	*Cymbeline.* The King's Men acquired the Blackfriars Playhouse.	
1610-11	*The Winter's Tale; The Tempest.* Shakespeare retired to Stratford.	*The Alchemist* (1610) by Ben Jonson.
1616	Shakespeare died, April 23.	
1623	The First Folio edition of Shakespeare's plays.	

Notes on the Editor and Contributors

DAVID BEVINGTON, editor of this volume, is Professor of English at the University of Virginia and Visiting Professor of English at the University of Chicago. He is author of *From "Mankind" to Marlowe* and of the forthcoming *Tudor Drama and Politics*.

PETER ALEXANDER, Regius Professor of English Language and Literature at Glasgow University from 1935 to 1963, is now Emeritus Professor. His publications include *Shakespeare's Life and Art, Hamlet: Father and Son,* and *Shakespeare*.

FREDSON BOWERS is Alumni Professor of English and Chairman of the Department at the University of Virginia. He is editor of *Studies in Bibliography*. His numerous publications include *Elizabethan Revenge Tragedy, Principles of Bibliographical Description,* an edition of *The Dramatic Works of Thomas Dekker,* and *Textual and Literary Criticism*.

A. C. BRADLEY (1851-1935) was Professor of Poetry at Oxford when he published *Shakespearean Tragedy* in 1904.

T. S. ELIOT was a Director of Faber and Faber, Ltd., in London, as well as a famous poet and critic. His literary studies include *The Sacred Wood, The Use of Poetry and the Use of Criticism, Elizabethan Essays,* and *Poetry and Drama*.

HARLEY GRANVILLE-BARKER (1877-1946) was, in addition to being a playwright and translator of plays, a distinguished lecturer in England and America. He delivered the Clark Lectures for 1930, the Cambridge Inaugural Lecture in 1934, the Presidental Address to the English Association, 1938, and many others. Among his publications are *The Companion to Shakespeare Studies* (with G. B. Harrison), *On Dramatic Method,* and several volumes of *Prefaces to Shakespeare*.

D. G. JAMES was Vice-Chancellor of the University of Southampton from 1952 to 1965; previously he was Winterstoke Professor of English and Dean of the Faculty of Arts at the University of Bristol. He has written much on Romantic and Victorian poets; his latest work is a study of *The Tempest*.

ERNEST JONES, a leading disciple of Sigmund Freud, pioneered the introduction of psychoanalysis into England and America. He resided in London until his death in 1958. Of his many monographs and editions, he is perhaps best known for *Sigmund Freud, Life and Work,* in three volumes.

BERTRAM JOSEPH teaches in the School of Drama at the University of Washington, Seattle. He specializes in the actor and his history, in studies that include *The Tragic Actor, Acting Shakespeare,* and *Elizabethan Acting.*

G. WILSON KNIGHT is now Emeritus Professor of English Literature at Leeds University, and has had considerable experience with the stage. His studies of Shakespeare include *The Imperial Theme, The Shakespearean Tempest,* and *The Crown of Life.*

L. C. KNIGHTS is King Edward VII Professor of English Literature at the University of Cambridge. Among other studies he has written *Drama and Society in the Age of Jonson* and *Some Shakespearean Themes.*

HARRY LEVIN is Irving Babbitt Professor of Comparative Literature at Harvard University. He is the author of *The Overreacher: A Study of Christopher Marlowe; Contexts of Criticism; The Power of Blackness: Hawthorne, Poe, Melville; The Gates of Horn: A Study of Five French Realists;* and other studies covering a wide range of literary interest.

C. S. LEWIS was, until his death in 1963, Professor of Medieval and Renaissance English at Cambridge University. He wrote science fiction, autobiography, and studies in Christian faith as well as literary criticism, and is perhaps best known for *The Allegory of Love, The Screwtape Letters,* and *English Literature in the Sixteenth Century.*

MAYNARD MACK is Sterling Professor of English and Chairman of the Department at Yale University. He is General Editor of Twentieth Century Views and Twentieth Century Interpretations, and is the author and editor of other works including *Pope and His Contemporaries* and *King Lear in Our Time.*

DON SALVADOR DE MADARIAGA of the College of Europe (Bruges), and Honorary Fellow of Exeter College, Oxford, has at various times been Spanish Ambassador to France and to the United States, and a diplomatic leader in the League of Nations. His many subjects of study include Shelley, Calderon, and *Don Quixote* as well as international relations.

THEODORE SPENCER was Boylston Professor of Rhetoric at Harvard University until his death in 1949. He published several volumes of poetry in addition to literary studies such as *Death and Elizabethan Tragedy* and *Shakespeare and the Nature of Man.*

ELMER EDGAR STOLL became Professor of English in 1915 at the University of Minnesota, where he taught for over forty years, pioneering the study of Shakespeare's Renaissance backgrounds. Among his many titles are *Art and Artifice in Shakespeare,* and *Shakespeare Studies, Historical and Comparative in Method.*

JOHN DOVER WILSON, formerly Regius Professor of Rhetoric and English Literature at the University of Edinburgh, has continued his prolific scholarly activity since his retirement from teaching. His works include *Life in Shakespeare's England, The Essential Shakespeare, The Fortunes of Falstaff,* and *Shakespeare's Happy Comedies.*

Selected Bibliography

This brief list should be considered supplementary to the complete volumes from which the selections in this collection have been chosen.

Bowers, Fredson T., *Elizabethan Revenge Tragedy, 1587-1642*. Princeton: Princeton University Press, 1940. A detailed study of the development of a dramatic type, from its background in popular attitudes and in Italianate revenge tradition, to its culmination during the period of *Hamlet,* and subsequent evolution.

Clemen, Wolfgang, *The Development of Shakespeare's Imagery*. London: Methuen & Co., Ltd., 1951. First published in 1936, this study avoids the extremes of those who find only image and symbol in Shakespeare, and offers instead a balanced, cautious, somewhat utilitarian appraisal of Shakespeare's "power to associate the imagery with the very fabric of the play"—the interplay between image and dramatic structure, staging, characterization, and the like.

Harrison, G. B., *Shakespeare's Tragedies*. London: Routledge & Kegan Paul, Ltd., 1951. A survey of the tragedies, useful as an introduction, with comments on numerous aspects of Shakespeare's dramaturgy such as versification, characterization, plot structure, Elizabethan staging, and the relevance of Shakespeare's contemporary world.

Kitto, H. D. F., *Form and Meaning in Drama*. London: Methuen & Co., Ltd., 1956. A study of *Hamlet* and six classical Greek dramas, with interesting comparative insights on the dramaturgy of the Greeks and the Elizabethans.

Ornstein, Robert, *The Moral Vision of Jacobean Tragedy*. Madison, Wis.: University of Wisconsin Press, 1960. An evaluation of the ethical viewpoint and artistic achievement of seventeenth-century tragedy, viewed against the political, cultural, and religious background of the age, and presenting Shakespeare's contribution in relation to a broad synthesis encompassing other major dramatists.

Rossiter, A. P., *Angel With Horns*. London: Longmans Green & Co., Ltd., 1961. A posthumously published collection of fifteen lectures delivered at Cambridge and Stratford, on *Hamlet* and other Shakespearean subjects— spirited, witty, learned, sometimes exasperatingly playful.

119

Spurgeon, Caroline, *Shakespeare's Imagery and What It Tells Us*. Cambridge, Eng.: Cambridge University Press, 1935. A landmark study of Shakespeare's imagery, based on exhaustive (although not infallible) methods of compilation and tabulation by which the author delineates the dominant image patterns for each play.

Stirling, Brents, *Unity in Shakespearean Tragedy*. New York: Columbia University Press, 1956. A study of "the interplay of theme and character" in *Hamlet* and six other tragedies; three chapters on *Hamlet* stress such unifying motifs as private consciousness probed crudely (as in the "recorder" episode with Rosencrantz and Guildenstern), and the "antic disposition" transforming both the hero and his dramatic environment.

Stoll, E. E., *Art and Artifice in Shakespeare*. Cambridge, Eng.: Cambridge University Press, 1933. A study of *Hamlet* and three other major tragedies by a leading apostle of historical criticism, interpreting Shakespeare as he was understood by his Elizabethan audience.

Tillyard, E. M. W., *Shakespeare's Problem Plays*. Toronto: University of Toronto Press, 1949. In the context of *Troilus and Cressida, All's Well That Ends Well,* and *Measure for Measure,* Tillyard controversially interprets *Hamlet* as a successful "problem" play concerned both with metaphysical issues and with problems of human nature.

Walker, Roy, *The Time Is Out of Joint: A Study of Hamlet*. London: A. Dakers, 1948. Against a background of universal corruption at the Danish court, the author sees Shakespeare's hero as "struggling toward the realization of order in human affairs," an order finally perceived in Hamlet's acceptance of providential destiny in his own death.